D1059209

Gail Siggelakis writes with the wit and wisdom that comes from loving people with care and concern. She deftly blends together the mental, emotional, and spiritual ingredients which shape relationships into intimate and wonderful connections. Her stories model the affirming way of life, and her information and practical applications encourage her readers to start anywhere on their journeys toward building satisfying relationships. An inviting and intimate read for all!

DR. NADINE HEITZ, director of counseling services, Rider University

Gail Siggelakis blends personal anecdotes, examples from popular culture as well as psychological research to provide the reader with a multi-course feast of ways to affirm and nourish relationships with ourselves, love ones, children, family, and co-workers. In the mental health field that all too often focuses on emotional pathology, this book offers a refreshing contrast that addresses ways to identify and support the underlying emotional health of those around us.

PETER A. CRIST, M.D., Medical orgone therapist, Stockton, New Jersey President, American College of Orgonomy, Princeton, New Jersey

This book validates the human need for affirming words. Through Gail's research, examples, personal stories, and strategies, readers can improve their relationships while engaging in more positive fulfilling lives. Hats off to Gail for reinforcing this critical human need.

CAROL KIVLER, speaker, author, and founder of
Courageous Recovery, LLC

The Affirming Way of Life *is a compelling 'How to' book that explores strategies to transform one's life, from negative to positive, by reconditioning your way of thinking and responding to others. Gail Siggelakis shows us that by affirming who we are, we can more readily accept ourselves and affirm the value of others. Her strategies are applicable for individuals at all levels—from pediatrics to geriatrics.*

CAV. DR. GILDA BATTAGLIA RORRO BALDASSARI,
former Director of the Office of Equal Educational Opportunity,
New Jersey Department of Education

The Affirming Way of Life *will make you think differently about the words you use and how you use them. Gail Siggelakis paints a compelling picture of how the things we say have resounding effects on the people who we cherish most. She challenges us to refine our language in order to uplift, embolden and empower those around us. Parents and educators who want the most for their children—a strong inner voice and a positive self-identity, need to read this book.*

RYAN LEE, Social Emotional Learning Specialist K-5 Schools and
co-owner of Master of Me Academy

The Affirming Way of Life

See the Good
Speak the Good
Spread the Good

Gail Siggelakis

Penny Lane Press
Trenton, New Jersey

Penny Lane Press
Trenton, New Jersey 08691
Theaffirmingwayoflife.com

© 2019 by Gail Siggelakis
Printed in the United States of America

Permissions gratefully acknowledged for quotes from the following copyrighted material:

Life in Motion: An Unlikely Ballerina by Misty Copeland, Copyright © 2014 Simon and Schuster; *Return to Love: Reflections on the Principles of A Course in Miracles,* Copyright © 1992 HarperPerennial; All TED and TEDx talks with title, speaker and year noted.

ISBN: 978-1-7336221-0-3
ISBN: 978-1-7336221-1-0 (ebook)

Editor's note:
The names, details, and circumstances may have been changed to protect the privacy of those mentioned in this book. This book is for information purposes only. It is not to serve as a substitute for professional medical advice. The publisher and the author disclaim liability for any medical outcomes that may occur as a result of applying the suggestions in this book.

Cover artwork by Sally Tazelaar
Cover graphics and interior design by Joni McPherson

To my mother, Selma
You deserve to be honored to the sky
for the gift of your loving heart
and affirming words.

Contents

Introduction

Do you long for more loving, warm-hearted relationships? Would you like to express more positive feelings to those you care about most? Then you've come to the right place. There's a resource you possess that can transform all your personal connections: *your words*. From the center of your heart, through the web of your thoughts, to the tip of your tongue, your words shape your relationships. *The Affirming Way of Life* will help you make the most of your words to bring greater joy to yourself and everyone in your life.

The words we speak to one another are a precious natural resource, more valuable than gold or diamonds. They require no financial outlay or extensive mining, and our supply is endless. Our words carry our thoughts and feelings that can bring unlimited love, delight, and support to everyone near or dear in our lives. Yet this essential resource for happy relationships is untapped by so many of us. Why? Because many of our parents and teachers never learned the life-impacting effect of their words. If they never learned it, how could they possibly teach us about it?

I discovered the gift of my words, by chance, on my fiftieth birthday. I awoke early to take stock of my accomplishments during my half-century of being. I looked closely at my life and felt quite disappointed. Though I was a devoted mother, wife, sister, and friend, and had taught elementary school

my entire adult life, I couldn't identify an outstanding talent
I possessed. I hadn't perfected any tangible skill like quilting
or gardening as some of my friends had, nor had I developed
the art of writing or music like others. I felt just plain
ordinary. And then it hit me! I was an outstanding affirmer.
I reflected on the frequent messages I received from people
in my life: "You always see the positives in others. You're so
generous with your compliments." And the sweetest part
of my discovery was that I had gotten this talent from my
bipolar mother, who, until that moment, I'd believed had
taught me only bad habits.

Though my mother spent half the year depressed in
bed, couldn't take care of our home, and never taught me
any concrete skills, she always noticed the positives in my
sister and me and never hesitated to express those loving
perceptions in a compliment. If I sewed a dress in home
economics class, she would tell me I had golden hands. If
I cooked a vegetarian dinner, she would say, "Oy, Gailie,
everything is so delicious. You're a great cook." I always had
her approval and felt valued and recognized in her eyes.
My mother unconsciously modeled for me the closeness
and pleasure that affirming brings. My mother's affirming
way of life became my own.

After my birthday realization, I began examining my
newly-recognized ability. Looking at my relationships with
the key people in my life, I noticed something wonderful:
My relationships with my husband, son, sister, and dearest
friends were very close, loving, and supportive. Of course
there are many variables that affect our connections, but I

had nurtured mine with abundant praise, perceived with eyes that saw the best in each person. People often commented on the closeness in our relationships. I also realized that during my thirty-eight years of teaching, my consistent affirming approach helped students grow and develop. It made them feel good about themselves and their talents, and I had long-lasting, warm-hearted relationships with many of them and their parents.

In the pages that follow, you will learn how to create warm, supportive, amazing relationships through affirming. You'll discover how affirming words create ripples of kindness that can impact people you don't even know. Here's what you'll find in the book:

- Each chapter begins with a personal story relating to the chapter theme.

- Next is an overview in *italics* of the key ideas in the chapter.

- Then comes the principles and practices.

- Each chapter ends with *Your Takeaways...*, a list of simple, specific actions you can take to begin living the ideas expressed in the chapter.

The Affirming Way of Life is presented in three parts:

Part One, The Foundation, introduces the new mindset and "speak set" with stories and examples that'll make you feel at home with affirming. Next, you'll find simple steps for developing the affirming habits that will vitalize your relationships. After that you'll learn about the destructive effects of criticism and how it lodges like bacteria in our brains. You'll also learn ways to express feelings and opinions without hurting others.

Part Two, The Forms of Affirming, gives you six different aspects of affirming:

- **Self-Supporting Words** – helps you start living the affirming way of life by first finding good words for yourself.

- **Recognition Words** – encourages you to notice the strengths in others and acknowledge those strengths.

- **Appreciative Words** – gets you in touch with heartfelt gratitude and the joy and benefits of expressing appreciation.

- **Encouraging Words** – guides you to offer hope to help others overcome challenges and achieve dreams.

- **Healing Words** – helps you find forgiveness for those who have wounded you. These words enable you to free up your heart energy and make room for more love.

- **Words for Our Children** – offers you ideas that encompass every form of affirming for those who need our words of praise the most—our children.

Part Three, The Send-Off, hones your ability to take compliments in. It leaves you with the importance of sharing the positives you see in others now, while you can.

As you read this book, your mind and heart will start opening to the pleasure and goodness that affirming can bring into your life, your relationships, and even beyond. By seeing the good in others and acknowledging them for it, you'll send ripples of positive energy into a world that is in dire need of kindness and care. You'll become a force for good.

Please be patient with yourself as you begin implementing the ideas in this book. Change takes time, so don't be disheartened if you feel uncomfortable or awkward at first. It's to be expected. Like learning a new language, learning a new way of thinking and acting can be both thrilling and intimidating at the same time.

Books have always been trusted friends that I turn to again and again for support as I take fledgling steps to change and grow. May this book be such a trusted friend to you. May it inspire you to keep moving forward on your journey to create a flow of good energy in all your relationships. I promise that choosing to more openly cherish those near and dear will make it possible to sweeten and deepen your relationships and open your life to ever-greater happiness.

PART ONE

the Foundation

Chapter 1

The Affirming Way of Life

Whenever my mother walked into someone's home the compliments flowed like honey. "Evie, you changed your living room furniture around. Ahh! The room looks so large and airy now. I love the way the couch faces the window into your yard. Now we can see all the birds fattening up at the birdfeeders!" And that was just a start. As Evie cooked dinner, my mother's compliments rolled off her tongue. "Ummm, your roast smells out of this world. You've got to give me your recipe." My mother was always welcome in her friends' homes because she brought kind words that made their days brighter. She had the gift of eyes that saw goodness and a heart that naturally overflowed. I call my mother's gift *the affirming way of life,* a phrase that not only became the title of this book, but also refers to the philosophy of living my mother gave me, and this book is meant to give you.

Ready to begin a life-changing adventure using words in wondrous ways to create more love and connections? Affirmations are words we speak that freshen stale relationships infusing them with good energy. The affirming way of life starts with an intentional mindshift from a focus on what's wrong with people to what's wonderful about them. Affirmations add warmth to relationships. In fact, they complete the old adage, "Actions speak louder than words." Those closest to you and even acquaintances will thrive on your encouraging words. And so will you! You will find that when you affirm the good in others the positives come back to you.

The Words We Speak Shape Our Relationships

As you embark on this life-changing journey, keep in mind that the words you speak help shape your relationships. To live the affirming way of life is to heighten your awareness of the gift or harm your words can bring to you and all those you care about and connect with.

We are social beings who live, work, and are part of a community of others. Our relationships impact us deeply and we equally impact those in our lives. It is in our relationships where we discover who we are and who we're not. It is through our relationships that we grow, make a difference in the world, and find personal meaning. And it is through our relationships that we suffer, are scarred, and learn to limit our sense of self. Language is our main tool for communicating with one another, thus the words we say are much more important than we often realize.

Affirmations Create Connection

My husband, Gus, is the youngest of seven, from a large, immigrant Greek family. It was an unwritten expectation that Gus, like his siblings, would marry within his culture—until my Jewish self came along and upset the apple cart. He hesitated to introduce me to his family for fear of their reaction, but after nine months of dating, he surprised me with a trip to Anavryti, his Greek mountain village six miles above Sparta. His oldest sister, Angie, and her husband, Billy, were traveling to Anavryti as well and ended up on the same flight with us.

When we arrived at Athens Airport, Angie hailed a taxi to transport us on the five-hour trip to their village. With suitcases overflowing from roof rack and trunk, and the delightful sound of Greek music playing on the radio, we headed for Gus's village.

As the taxi rolled into the palm-tree-lined streets of Sparta, we were greeted with shouts and people running up to the car yelling, "Angie, Angie, Angie!" to which she replied, laughing, "Yasou! Ti kaneis, agape mou?" (Hello! How are you my love?) I felt like I was with a celebrity.

"Angie, I think you're the Sophia Loren of Greece," I declared in true awe. "You're famous here."

"Oh, come on, Gail. They're just friends and cousins who are happy to see me," she responded with obvious pleasure.

The next day Gus and I sat at Angie and Billy's kitchen table with their friends from the village. Angie served us stuffed grape leaves with the creamiest lemon sauce, lahana (boiled dandelion greens and bright orange zucchini flowers drizzled with olive oil), and pork chops grilled with mountain oregano. Plates of kalamata olives, feta cheese, and fresh bread completed the feast. I relished every bite.

"I never tasted anything as delicious as this," I said. "You're a fabulous cook, Angie. Would you teach me how to make some Greek dishes?"

"All right, all right," she laughed, and proceeded to describe in wonderful detail how her neighbor grew and cured the olives, how the dandelion greens must be picked young and tender in the early morning, and how in order to make the sauce for the grape leaves she had to create the just right blend of eggs, lemon, and juices from the pot.

Looking back, I can see how my open admiration helped Angie feel my acceptance, approval, and appreciation. I remember how she offered me the same enthusiastic acceptance as we walked around the village. She'd hold my arm, and with her charming twinkle, say to villagers we'd encounter, "This is my brother's girlfriend, Gail. She's not fussy. She eats everything. Even if she wasn't with my brother, I'd love her." My expressed enjoyment of Angie opened a connection between us that has deepened throughout the years.

Will affirming always open the way for a bond between you and others? Not necessarily. You won't especially want to get closer to everyone you compliment, but affirming will make your moments with others sweeter as givers and receivers.

Blow Away the Dust

Everyday living can make us forget the sweetness we've shared with significant others. With so much on our minds and so much to do, we sometimes forget how important our loved ones are to us. They can become like a beloved book on the shelf, a great story we once raved about that now sits unrecognized, gathering dust.

To Kill a Mockingbird was the best book I ever read, yet it's been years since I've thought about the richness it brought into my life. My beloved copy sat dusty and neglected on my bookshelf. When the author, Harper Lee, died in 2016, discussions about her and her characters abounded on TV, and all of a sudden I remembered what Scout, Atticus, and the entire book meant to me. *To Kill a Mockingbird* came alive again in my heart and mind.

I'm sorry to say, I did the same thing with my husband. When Gus and I were dating, I adored everything about him and my words of appreciation streamed steadily. But over time, the demands of everyday life and a growing list of grievances, saw my steady stream of praise diminish into drips and drops, like a faucet with a slow leak. My wake-up moment came the day he said, "You always talk about how wonderful the people you work with are, but I don't hear a word of appreciation about me."

My affirmer-self felt ashamed. True is true. I'd been treating Gus like my dusty copy of *To Kill a Mockingbird*. I needed to make amends. At first I felt rusty complimenting him. I had to ask myself, *What would be missing from my life if Gus weren't there?* The obvious, everyday things came to mind first: he paid our bills, maintained our cars, often did the laundry, washed the dishes, fixed everything. *Wow,* I thought, *I'm really fortunate.* Then I thought about what he brought to me emotionally and spiritually: he accepted and appreciated me despite my neuroticisms, he encouraged me to pursue my dreams, and he always saw me as youthful as a twenty-year-old. There was so much good he brought into my life that I'd been taking for granted. So the next time I came home and found my underwear and socks washed and folded, I said, "Honey, you're the best. I am *so* lucky to have a husband who does the laundry."

"No problem," he said, with a little grin.

We had just pulled out of our neighborhood on a trip to New York City when I realized I'd done my usual forgetting of something. I said, "Would you turn around? I forgot my sunglasses."

He responded good-naturedly, "Why should this trip be any different from all our others," and did a quick U-turn.

"Gussie, I so appreciate your flexibility and understanding. How many other husbands would turn around without a complaint?"

"No problem, you don't complain when I'm late for dinner so why should I complain when you're forgetful?"

My continued expression of appreciation over time led to Gus's reciprocal compliments. Before long our relationship

felt revived and enlivened, bringing us greater joy and closeness and even rippling out to the way we connected with
others in our lives.

Our relationships can bring far more joy when we take
them off the shelf of familiarity, blow away the dust, and appreciate the wonder again. But how do we get to that place?

Mindshift

We often become mired in unresolved grievances with the
people we're closest to. What isn't talked through between
people can linger and grow into an ugly beast. The main
reason I was rusty at complimenting Gus was my laundry
list of unmet expectations and complaints. As wonderful
as Gus seemed when I brainstormed all the good he'd
brought into my life, my list of dissatisfactions with him
screamed even louder: *He doesn't help with Theo's school issues.*
I'm drowning in them. He doesn't let me express my anger. I can't
be real with him. He gets moody often and won't talk. Sometimes I
feel shut out. Stewing in all my grievances dulled Gus's initial
shine as much as seemingly imperceptible dust settles on a
mirror and dims what we see. My negative thoughts colored
him gray, and over time a wide gulf formed between us.

The turning point came when I saw a movie about a
couple much like us who'd lost their intimacy and connection. It was so painful to watch that I left the theatre
trembling with the voice in my head insisting, *I must talk to*
Gus; I can't ignore this truth.

That night, shaking as if chilled, fearing my words
might shut Gus down as they so often did, I spoke to

him. "I saw a movie today about a couple who were living completely separate lives—and they were us. I can't take it the way we are."

His response surprised me. "I feel the same way."

We talked for hours, and discovered that we each did our own thing every night because the other was occupied—with TV or the phone. It wasn't an easy conversation, but what came out of it was that we both wanted a closer, more fulfilling relationship with each other. We brainstormed a list of things we mutually enjoyed doing and bit by bit began having more fun together.

Before our pivotal conversation, all I could see was the layer of dust. I realized if I was going to save my marriage, I had to let go of my attitudes toward Gus to see that he was still my treasured copy of *To Kill a Mockingbird*.

Many of us do this. We judge, we criticize, we compare, we nurture our discontent. Perhaps not with everyone, and not at all times; but seeing the negative in people we're close to is all too common. *My wife needs to lose weight. My daughter is lazy. My friend is so full of herself. I suck at this.* Our thoughts are like magnets. Whatever we focus on draws more of the same to us. One negative thought leads to another, and before we know it our brain is stuck on the negative south pole of the magnet and can't seem to budge.

I don't want to oversimplify the process of releasing negative emotions. There are root causes for some negative emotions that deserve to be explored, possibly with the help of a good therapist. Nevertheless, living the affirming way of life helps us choose to focus our thoughts on the positive in others. When I created my list of what would be missing from my life if Gus weren't in it, I was creating an intentional mindshift. Even after our relationship-renewing conversation, my positive thoughts felt tenuous—not that real or strong. But when I voiced them to Gus and saw the glimmer of happiness on his face, the positive north end of the magnet began its magic pull upward. The more I affirmed Gus, the more positive I felt about him and the more positively he responded to me. Those old loving feelings began flooding my heart again.

Neuropsychologist Rick Hanson, in his book *Hardwiring Happiness,* says that our brains have evolved from our caveman ancestors who had to learn quickly from bad experiences or they could become a saber-toothed tiger's dinner. We continue to harbor their negative bias as a survival mechanism, but the good news is we also possess the power to shift to the positive. When we savor positive experiences for ten seconds or more, Hanson says we literally install those experiences in our brain, strengthening the centers that retain those feelings.

This is what installing looks like when it comes to tending the flow of positive feelings toward my husband: I think, *It was so kind of Gus to fold my exercise clothes and put them away. He was really happy when I affirmed him for it. Way to go, Gail!* Later, as I get ready for bed, I smile and say to myself, *You're putting the love back into your relationship.* I savor the effect of my expressed appreciation on each of us, and soak in the good feelings my mindshift has created. The process of affirming not only feels good, it actually makes the brain happier.

Add Warmth

I much prefer to be with people who affirm and appreciate me than those who don't. The people I'm close to—my confidants, my loved ones—are generous with praise. I know they adore and value me because they tell me so. I feel most relaxed and at home with them. They add warmth to my life.

It's not that I can't have good relationships with people who don't affirm me; I just don't feel as accepted and appreciated. I don't feel the warmth. How about you? Who do you prefer to be with? What is it about your relationship with those people that makes you comfortable and happy?

In *The 5 Love Languages,* marriage expert, Gary Chapman says that each of us has one of the following primary ways we get the message that we are loved from others: spending quality time together, receiving gifts, through acts of service, physical touch, and words of affirmation. Gary encourages us to understand our spouse's love language for a long-lasting fulfilling marriage. What he says makes sense, but I think we can take it a step further. I believe any relationship becomes closer when we verbally express our positive feelings towards the other person. As I started focusing on the good I appreciated in my husband and telling him, he reciprocated with me. Although expressing words of affirmation wasn't as natural for Gus, the more I affirmed him, the more expressive he became with me. Our closeness is now tangible.

One of my favorite movies is *About Time.* In it, Tim, a member of a quirky close-knit British family, discovers on his twenty-first birthday that the men in his family can travel back through time to change their actions and improve their futures. He uses this special power to meet and marry Mary. At their wedding, his father gives the best man speech. "I've only loved three men in my life," he says, "Uncle Desmond, BB King, and Tim." Time passes, and Tim's dad dies. After the funeral, Uncle Desmond, elderly, sweet, and slightly mentally challenged, says "At your wedding, your dad said he loved me. That was probably the best day of my life." *The best day of his life.* That is how much affirming words mean. What also made the moment sad was the fact that until that day, Tim's dad hadn't voiced those words. Uncle Desmond had missed out on the real warmth his brother-in-law felt for him.

Action's Best Friend

A post on Facebook gave me pause to think: Winnie the Pooh and Piglet were walking paw-in-paw into the sunset with this message written underneath, "Love isn't what you say. Love is what you do." It reminded me of the adage, "Actions speak louder than words." And I thought, *something's missing here.*

Yes, the actions of others definitely show how much they value us, but the problem is the phrase overlooks the importance of words. In *About Time*, Tim's dad always acted with kindness and care toward Uncle Desmond, but Uncle Desmond didn't realize his brother-in-law's feelings because they were never *said.* Hearing "I love you" made all the difference in the world to Uncle Desmond.

Words of appreciation, admiration, and enjoyment confirm that we matter and are valued by those in our lives. They don't leave us wondering where we stand.

When I retired from teaching, one of my teammates said, "You inspire me to be better." I was touched and amazed because in our more than thirty years of friendship, she had never once spoken to me of my impact on her. Her words made me feel valued and closer to her. I felt the warmth. There's something missing in the adage, "Actions speak louder than words," and what's missing is, "Words from the *heart* make relationships *heartier*."

Be a Fan

A tragic accident happened recently in my town. A seventeen-year-old girl was driving to school for an early morning field trip when she hit and killed our school superintendent while he was out for his early morning jog. Steve was youthful, high-minded, devoted to his family, the community, and his faith, and had a smile that glowed from within. He was beloved by all. At his funeral, his wife and three handsome young adult sons encapsulated his legacy in the most touching inspiring tribute I'd ever heard.

His oldest son, Ryan, captured his father's essence in five words, "My dad was a fan."

"Though my dad was an athlete and into sports, he was not the kind of fan you'd think. He was a fan of the people he cared about. He was a fan of me and my brothers, whether we won a game or lost. He was a fan of my mother,

celebrating her successes and encouraging her to grow beyond her limits. And he was a fan of all my friends, interested in everything in their lives."

Ryan described his dad's presence at games and every
activity, and the words of praise his dad gave freely, win or
lose. When his team lost a lacrosse tournament, his dad
gave him a warm hug and said, "I loved watching you play,
Son. You had some good dodges on the field today. You
put your heart into the game; that's all you can do." From
both actions and words, Ryan felt his dad's loving support
and belief in him.

Ryan ended his eulogy with a message to all: "Be like
my dad. Be a fan of the people who matter most to you."

Living the affirming way of life is about being a fan.
Our actions and words show those who matter most to us,
who they are, and that they are valued and loved *because* of
who they are. There is no greater gift we can offer them.

I've been a lifelong fan of my son, Theo, and it hasn't
always been easy. Before Theo turned three, he was thrown
out of every child care setting he attended for impulsivity—
biting, kicking, and throwing things. School was no better.
Every year teachers reported that he would call out, disrupt
their class, and that he didn't pay attention. It turned out
Theo had ADHD. I did everything I could to work with
his teachers, but found it painful to receive continuous
negative feedback about my boy. As his fan, I knew he was
so much more than their negative labels.

My eyes saw the bigger picture of who my son really was.
I loved his sparkle and easygoing personality, his insights,

clever humor, and passionate focus on his interests. As his mother, if I didn't see the good in him, who would?

Gus and I learned to deal with Theo's challenges, while also reveling in his sterling traits. As of this writing, Theo is twenty-seven, and we see the payoff of affirming the good in him. He is a confident, successful, good person, and our fan too.

Make Someone's Day

After Ryan's eulogy, Steve's second son, Shaun, told his story about his dad. "Every morning as I was leaving for school my dad would say, 'make someone's day.'" Shaun's father made him aware of making a difference in the lives of others. Even the people we don't have a fan relationship with need our kind words. The cashier at the grocery store, the repair person, the secretary at the office, your child's teacher, a co-worker—our words matter to them all. Our compliments may provide the uplift or support to someone when they need it most.

I love Denise's Pilates/yoga class at my gym because she always wears a wide, happy grin, is very human, and laughs a lot. The other day, after class, I went up to her as she was rolling up her purple yoga mat and said, "Denise I just love your class. You have such a warm smile and such good energy. Thank you."

"You made my day!" she said and we shared a happy glow.

My sister, Lois, is the kindest most compassionate person I know. She is a passionate diabetes educator who works long hours. We often talk about how much it means to be acknowledged for making a difference—how it fuels our fire. Each day Lois meets with at least seven patients. She listens to their challenges, then comforts, encourages, and guides with a full heart. The other day she told me the following story:

"At the end of the day, David, our nurse practitioner, said, 'I was just telling a new patient that we have the best diabetes educator in the state, and that she's going to be so lucky to work with you.' Then Egles, our endocrinologist, chimed in, 'That's right and I always tell patients that you're my spiritual guide.' I can't get over how these two great men think so highly of me! I feel so valued and respected." Their acknowledgement had made her day.

A Gift for Yourself

My home environment growing up was saturated with my mother's depression and my father's perfectionism. As a self-doubting worrier, always waiting for the other shoe to drop, I sought help through therapy, spiritual practices, and life-changing conversations with friends. The gray cloud of my life eventually lifted, and I could see after my fiftieth birthday epiphany that living my mother's way of noticing the good in others and affirming them for it, helped me tip the balance scale of my thoughts from negative to positive. It helped me become optimistic.

In their book, *Words Can Change Your Brain,* neuroscientists Andrew Newberg, M.D. and Mark Robert Waldman talk about how words can counteract the brain's built-in negativity. The longer we focus on positive words, the more our brain centers begin to change. The parietal lobe reshapes, affecting our perceptions of self and others. Over time the thalamus—which controls sensing—changes the way we see reality. Focusing on the good in ourselves and others and verbalizing these perceptions, actually reshapes the brain to perceive life more positively.

Here's a typical morning when I was teaching, experienced through the affirming frame of mind. I see Cheryl, a teacher's aide, entering my school. "You have a new haircut. I love it," I tell her. She beams, unloads her doubts about it and gives me a big hug. My words fuel our heart connection.

Next, I stop by my friend Kathy's room. She tells me about her frustration with a flawed, new granite counter installed in her kitchen. I can tell she's not clear about what to do. "You're persistent and honest," I tell her. "If it's not what you ordered, speak up. You always get results when you do."

"Thanks, Gail. Your words make me feel more confident." She decides to call the installer. My affirmation buoys Kathy's spirits, inspires her to action, and uplifts us both.

My teammate Janet is in our classroom when I arrive. She's put a playful snowman image and instructions on our computerized whiteboard to greet our students. I smile at her and say, "You are the best! What would I do without you! I so appreciate you getting things ready. I feel like I can put my feet up and just shoot the breeze!"

"Aw, it's nothing, Gailie," she quips as we share a good laugh. I can see she feels valued, and I feel lucky to have her. My words make us both feel good.

Affirmations put us all in a positive frame of mind. Every message we relay to others gets installed in our own brains too. And if nothing else in our day goes well for us, we're still uplifted by seeing that our words really do make a difference to others.

The Unsaid

When our school superintendent died, Heather, the parent of a former student, wrote this on Facebook: "So tragic!! It was an honor to have worked with such a wonderful man who was clearly full of passion about education. Last time I saw him he was picking up pizza at a local restaurant. I told him how much his new teacher orientation had meant to me years back. I'm so grateful I was able to thank him. Don't wait to tell someone what an impact they've had on you because you may never get the chance!"

How often do we feel gratitude or admiration for another person, but don't seize the moment to let them know? We think we're too busy, too shy, or they already know how we feel. We tell ourselves it's not that important. But it is!

My Uncle Marty, my father's younger brother, was a second father to me. Last summer he wasn't feeling himself. He complained of stomach pains and could barely eat. My cousin lived hours away and asked if I could take her dad to his doctor's appointment. I was more than happy to help because Uncle Marty was the easiest and most supportive elder in my family. He called me every week, and always remembered my birthday with cards full of praise. When he came to our house for a holiday dinner, he would call the next morning to rave about the meal. I adored him.

As we sat in the waiting room, arm in arm, I reminded Uncle Marty how much I loved and appreciated him.

"You are the best uncle. I love that we can sit together and talk about everything. I always appreciate when you say, 'Love you, too, Dear,' at the end of every phone call. I'm so lucky to have you."

"I'm lucky to have you too, Dear," he replied. And that was it. A few days later he was in the hospital with pancreatic cancer, unable to communicate or respond. Uncle Marty passed away within three weeks. I was so grateful to have had one more chance to let my sweet uncle know how much he meant to me.

Life is fleeting. Living the affirming way of life enables us to develop the habit of expressing what's in our heart *now*. Then there's no need to worry about words left unsaid.

Your Takeaways

1. **Recognize affirming words strengthen your relationships and create bonds of connection, care, and mutual appreciation.**

2. Focus on all that's good in the people in your life. Become a fan.

3. Affirm those closest to you daily. Notice the pleasure it brings to each of you.

4. Live by the adage: Words from the heart make relationships heartier.

CHAPTER 2

Developing the Affirming Habit

Staff meetings after a full day of teaching were always grueling. As I sat in the media center dreading the next mandate in our already overflowing must-do list, I was delighted to see that the presenter was one of my teammates. Rob started with a big smile, then cracked jokes that made everyone laugh and loosen up. *Wow*, I thought. *Rob seems so comfortable in a leadership role.* His topic on the use of an online grade book gave me stomach cramps, but he made it seem doable. My thoughts went something like this: *Rob has come such a long way.* (He was in his fourth year of teaching, surviving two years of challenging fifth-grade students.) *I'm always impressed with all the thought he puts into his lessons, and it's so wonderful that he's happy to share his computer savvy. Rob definitely has leadership potential.*

It was the first time he presented to the staff, and he probably was a little nervous. The next morning I decided to stop by Rob's classroom. "You're a natural leader! I couldn't get over how comfortable you seemed during your presentation yesterday. Loved your jokes and the way you explained the online grade book. You'd make an excellent principal someday. You have a lot to offer children and teachers."

"Thanks," he said, his face shining. "I really appreciate that. I wasn't sure if I made sense. Principal? Wow, hadn't thought of that. Thanks for coming in. You made my day." It was a powerful moment for both of us.

Developing the affirming habit begins with a desire for more connection in our relationships. The goal is to appreciate ordinary everyday kindnesses and sterling qualities in others we may have overlooked. From this place of appreciation our affirmations can flow. An easy-to-follow approach uses the Four S's—Simple, Specific, Skills-based, and Sincere—in tone and in words. Practice makes affirming become second nature. Start with rituals such as birthdays, holidays, graduations, or weddings, embracing these events as opportunities to affirm people verbally or in writing. Then branch out into everyday life. Be patient with the process— you are building a life-long habit.

Extraordinary Ordinary—What's the Good Here

One of my favorite stories is "The Fir Tree " by Hans Christian Anderson. It features a young tree in the forest that
imagines the greatness that lies ahead for all the tall trees
when they're cut down. He too wants to become the mast of
a ship, a beautiful piece of furniture, or a beloved Christmas
tree. Sadly though, dreaming ahead robs him of the gifts of
the moment: sunlight bathing him with warmth, squirrels
playing amidst his branches, birds singing beautiful melo-
dies. Reality strikes when his time to be felled arrives. For
one short night he is adored as a Christmas tree, but then
quickly forgotten. A few days later he is dragged up to the
dark attic and left to pine for his former ordinary pleasures.

Humans can be so much like the fir tree. Our thoughts
are often so consumed with future tasks, or occupied with
past grievances, that we don't notice the ordinary goodness
of the moment. I know, because there was a time when I
was the fir tree. This is how my thinking used to be: A loyal
friend would call to see how I was doing after a stressful
week and I'd say to myself, *she's got nothing better to do.* My
husband would scrape the ice off my windshield and I'd
think, *he's just car focused.* A co-worker would compliment
me on the way I communicated with my students and I'd
reflect, *I always hear the same old thing.*

Unlike the fir tree, though, I seized the opportunity to
change my way of thinking. Over time, I learned to put my
attention on the good in the small everyday occurrences of
life, as though scanning for hidden treasures with a metal

detector. Ordinary kindnesses have become a source of joy for me and they can do the same for you.

If Gus agrees to go shopping with me, even though I know it's the last thing he wants to do, I think, *wow, he cares more about pleasing me than his own satisfaction. I'm lucky.* If my son, Theo, tells me about a frustrating disagreement he had, I think, *I'm so happy my son wants to share his thoughts and feelings with me.* If I drop my glove in the mall and a stranger returns it, I think, *it's amazing how kind people can be.*

Seeing the good in people and asking, *what's the good here?* is the clay that can be molded into affirming words. Pause after time spent with other people and ask yourself:

- What made me happy about our time together?

- In what way is this person kind?

- What do I enjoy about her?

- What were the ways he was helpful?

- What do I admire about her?

- What goodness does this person add to life?

How to Affirm with the Four S's

Below is an easy-to-follow approach to guide you in crafting affirmations. I've simplified the process into four aspects of affirming. The first, Simple, is to help you get started with someone who's easy for you to affirm, and a simple way to find the words to say. The next three S's—Specific, Skills-based, and Sincere, will help you focus your thoughts and words when you affirm.

1. Simple

Start your practice with someone who is easy to affirm—maybe a family member, a dear friend, or a kind co-worker; perhaps a friendly store clerk.

- Ask yourself, *"What's the good here?"* Take a breath, then be bold and tell the person what you notice or value about him.

Kathy, who volunteered to try out the ideas in the book because she saw all the warmth that affirming created in my life, chose to start with her husband, Harold. She loves and appreciates him dearly, but rarely tells him. "Harold, you're always there for me, I don't know what I'd do without you."

She explained how she chose the words. "I was thinking about how Harold listened so patiently last night when I was really upset about something. I realized he's always in my corner."

Kathy reported that Harold responded with a big happy smile, saying, "Of course! You're my girl." She added, "Saying positive things to him got me to focus on the good he does instead of the things that annoy me."

Wayne chose to affirm his four-year-old daughter Penny—a more comfortable place for him to start with than adults. He described her as headstrong, incredibly smart, and a wiz with words. One night Penny was explaining to him why children should decide their own bedtime. "Daddy," she said, "you always let me make choices about books and games, so why not bedtime?"

"I couldn't get over how clever she was to use my parenting technique to get what she wanted," Wayne explained. "I said to her, 'Parents decide bedtimes because we know what's healthy for you, but you are very convincing. You'd make a great lawyer someday.'"

By asking himself "What's the good here?" Wayne shifted from being annoyed with his daughter to focusing on building her sense of self.

If affirming feels awkward, start by passing on compliments from others. It's simpler than coming up with your own, and you still become the bearer of gifts. My teammate Marie recently retired after teaching elementary school for forty-four years. An acquaintance commented to me that she saw Marie at the gym and that she looked more relaxed and fit than ever. The next time I saw Marie I passed on the compliment and added, "Retirement seems to agree with you." Repeating a compliment from someone else was an easy way to share joy and connection with a friend.

 Who might you feel comfortable affirming? Start an affirmation notebook with your easy-to-affirm person as the first name in it. The other three S's that follow will give you ideas to jot down to help you meaningfully affirm your chosen person and may get you thinking of affirmations for others, too. (Note: Throughout the book there will be italicized questions to get you to reflect and act on the ideas presented. You will have many opportunities to use your affirmation notebook.)

2. Specific

My mother's affirming way of being always made me feel loved, but surprisingly it didn't build my confidence. She would frequently say, "Gailie, you're so handy," no matter what I did, big or small. My mother's younger sister, Aunt Lil, who was like a second mother to me, would often say, "You're no ordinary girl. You deserve to marry someone special like you." I knew I was loved and valued, but their compliments sometimes had the opposite effect of what you'd expect—they made me doubt myself.

When my mother said I was so handy, I thought of all the ways I was careless, and of people who could do things better than me. When Aunt Lil said I was extraordinary, I felt pressure to be something greater than I knew how to be. The problem with their generalized praise was it didn't give me anything specific to identify within myself. It was too big to live up to, so negative self-talk filled in the gap. This is what happens to many of us when we receive generalized compliments. The work of Adele Faber and Elaine Mazlish helped me understand what was missing in my mother's and aunt's praise. In an *American Federation of Teachers Journal* article, "Praise That Doesn't Demean, Criticism That Doesn't Wound," Faber and Mazlish say compliments that reach the heart and mind of the receiver:

- are specific, and

- describe in detail what the person did well, so that the person can recognize it and internally praise himself, too.

Had my mother named a specific way I was handy such as, "You're great with the sewing machine. I'm impressed with the way you sewed together your sister's ripped blanket," I might have thought, Yes, I am able to sew and use my skill to help my sister. If Aunt Lil had said, "I admire the way you constantly read self-help books to better handle your life," I might have thought, I am a person who takes actions to make my life better.

Glowing generalized words still have a place in our compliments—when we're moved to express our love. When my neighbor turned fifty, her husband threw her a surprise birthday party. As we all gathered around, he gently placed a crown on her head and said, "You are my princess always." Throwing her arms around his neck she exuberantly said, "You are the most wonderful husband in the world!" Glowing praise.

During a class play, one of my students had the audience in stitches. Afterwards, I overheard his mother say to him as she ruffled his hair, "You're so talented!" Joy beamed from both their faces.

Generalized and specific compliments each have their place in building others up and sharing loving feelings. The gift of specific praise is that it can help others identify particular strengths that become anchors for a positive sense of self.

What do you specifically admire, respect, or appreciate in the person you're choosing to affirm? Write it down and refer to it to help you create your affirmations.

3. Skills-based

Of course, there are endless things we can appreciate about the people in our lives. Here's a list of skills and personal qualities you might want to zero in on as you hone your affirming skills. Use the list as a starting point.

- **Relationship Skills** – Being sensitive to the feelings of others; being perceptive, kind, caring, understanding, compassionate, supportive.

- **Personal Skills** – Being flexible, reflective, honest, growth-oriented, easy-going, funny, playful, bubbly, enthusiastic, hard-working, determined, motivated, insightful, resilient, patient, respectful; having high standards and integrity.

- **Physical Skills** – Being athletic, mechanical, strong, healthy, energetic; having endurance.

- **Business/Work-related Skills** – Being organized, articulate, analytical, thorough, dependable, assertive, efficient, creative, a team player, a good listener, a skilled negotiator, a strong leader.

Lynn was interested in developing the affirming habit and chose to appreciate her son-in-law Brian for his kindness and care. He not only took her to the hospital when her husband had surgery, he also stayed with her. She said, "It's so caring of you to stay with me the whole time. Your presence makes me feel so comforted and taken care of." Brian's pleasure in receiving her affirmation was obvious in his response:

"You're like a mother to me. I'm happy to be here with you."

Lynn told me that normally she would have just thanked Brian, but after reading my manuscript, she was prompted to think deeper about Brian's actions and feelings. She wanted to acknowledge him more specifically.

Joe focused on a trait he admired in someone at work. "Hey, Bill, thanks for bringing up to the project leader that our input was not considered. You are an assertive dude." He valued his co-worker's willingness to put himself on the line. Joe and Bill went out for drinks afterward and brainstormed their next steps to propel their ideas forward.

 Are there skills or qualities you'd like to add to your list of what you appreciate in the person you're choosing to affirm?

4. Sincere

Living the affirming way of life is about speaking from your heart to touch the hearts of others. We affirm, in part, to put good energy into our relationships. Asking, "What's the good here?" helps us access important feelings that might have otherwise gone unrecognized. We never know the wonder that might come out of focusing on the positives in others and telling them.

A relationship that transformed my life developed as a result of sincere words. Ryan and I were teammates during the last five years of my teaching career. Once a month we gathered our six fifth-grade classes together for a recognition assembly. Each teacher acknowledged the efforts and growth of two students in the presence of their peers. Ryan's words of recognition inspired his students, along with every child and adult in the room.

After one such assembly, we were walking our students back to our classrooms and I said to Ryan, "I was totally blown away by the way you acknowledged Brandon. It was so powerful to hear you say, 'Like Brandon, you too can choose to make the most of your time by bringing your focused attention and determination to everything you do. You are choosing a way of life.' You amaze me, Ryan. Your words are so inspiring. You have a gift of motivating others to rise to their highest selves."

"Wow, thanks Gail," he answered, smiling. "I really appreciate you saying that."

A deep connection began blooming between us that day. This connection motivated me to run a half marathon and write this book—things I didn't imagine possible before Ryan's inspiring influence. He once told me that the sincerity of my words drew him to me and gave him more confidence to teach his students the subject he really believed in—self-knowledge. Our relationship continues to be a joy and mutual gift.

My son, Theo, has a business that depends on establishing relationships with a large network of people. He has found that offering sincere compliments opens doors. When he heard that Robert would be an excellent go-to guy for his new project, Theo called him with an invitation to lunch. "I heard you're the guy I need to meet because you know everyone and everything about New Jersey politics." Theo's honest acknowledgement opened the way for a business relationship that's still going strong.

Whatever our motive for affirming, whether to encourage, open the door to a relationship, or just create positive feelings, speaking from the heart with sincerity is more likely to be well-received. And the beauty of it is each time we touch another's heart we add positive ripples into the world.

Develop Rituals

Any celebration of the people in your life can be made sweeter and more meaningful with affirmations. Birthdays, graduations, holidays, engagements, showers, weddings are all opportunities to make the moment more precious with words from the heart that recognize the people being honored and the significance of the event.

A team of teachers I worked with became closer when we developed an affirming ritual. To celebrate each other's birthdays, we treated the birthday person to lunch. We'd often chat about school and our families, but rarely acknowledged the lunch was a celebration. I suggested using our words as the guest of honor's gift, sharing how much we admired and appreciated her. Our first occasion was Phyllis's birthday.

After some initial awkwardness, the compliments flowed:

"You touch my heart the way you take such joy in any good news I share with you."

"You listen to all of us with your whole heart. You're such a good person."

"You are a wonderful teacher. I admire the way you plan so many fun hands-on activities for your science lessons."

By the time we all took a turn, Phyllis was grinning from ear-to-ear. "I don't know what to say. I love you guys. You made me feel so valued. I never thought there was anything special about me. This is the best birthday present ever. Thank you all so much."

We can extend this ritual to everyone in our lives. Whether through phone calls, greeting cards, or over a celebratory meal, we can express how much we value the people we care about. Any milestone is more precious when we express words of pride, joy, admiration, and appreciation.

Strengthening the Habit

Research says it takes at least sixty-six days practicing a new behavior to have it become automatic. When my brother-in-law George was coaching my nieces in basketball, he had them take 250 shots a day. Practice. A successful pianist I know plays the piano at least three hours a day. Practice. Lucky for us, there are plenty of people we can practice affirming with.

The people you live with are a great place to start. If you live alone, reach out and affirm a friend or relative through a phone call, a text, or an email. I'm sure the cashier at the grocery store or the librarian would appreciate receiving some positive words, as would the people you work with.

Each time you affirm someone record it in your affirming way of life notebook. As the string of entries lengthens, the habit of affirming grows. Hang note cards with your goal of affirming others in places you're sure to look—the bathroom mirror, a closet shelf, a bulletin board over your desk, the refrigerator. (I find visual reminders essential to developing habits.) You might also post note cards with thoughts supporting your affirming mind shift. Here are a few to get you started:

- I'm awakening to the ordinary goodness right before my eyes.

- With everyone I see I ask, "What's the good here?"

- The more good I notice in others, the more good I see in myself.

- Affirming brings love and joy to my relationships and my life.

- I am spreading positive energy in the world.

Create note cards reminding you to affirm people daily:

- I affirm people I care about at least once a day.

- When I notice something positive about co-workers, friends, or neighbors, I tell them.

- I pass on compliments.

- I use the four S's of affirming and keep my acknowledgements simple, specific, skills-based, and sincere.

Some other ways to remind yourself to affirm are:

- Set affirming as a reminder in your phone.

- Put affirming on a daily to-do list.

- Write a reminder on your calendar.

Adopt a way that works for you to make strengthening your affirmation habit your own—something you can do every day. Don't be surprised if you find that the flow of good energy your new habit brings becomes your greatest reinforcement.

Your Takeaways

1. **Notice the extraordinary, ordinary gifts others bring into your life.**

2. **Affirm daily those near and dear.**

3. **Affirm with the four S's—simple, specific, skills-based, sincere.**

4. **Pass on compliments.**

5. **Develop affirming rituals to recognize important milestones in your family and friends' lives.**

6. **Create and use reminders that work for you.**

CHAPTER 3

Criticism—Affirming's Natural Associate

When I was twenty-one my parents divorced and my dad remarried. It was a very unsettling time of my life. I had just graduated from college with no career direction. Aunt Lil convinced me to return home and live with my mother to give her support since she was so depressed. I felt rudderless and adrift in a dark sea.

My dad's new wife, Eleanor, was a cosmopolitan New Yorker, snappy in style and comment, yet eager to be accepted by my sister and me. One evening shortly after their marriage, they invited us into Manhattan for dinner so we could get to know each other better.

"What kind of work are you going to do now that you've graduated?" Eleanor asked me.

"I'm not really sure. With my early childhood major, the only thing I'm prepared to do is teach preschool." I felt raw and vulnerable.

Eleanor quickly retorted, "You seem quite immature for your age. When I graduated college I went right to work at the Ted Mack's *Original Amateur Hour*. And my daughter Lana, she knows exactly what she's going to do when she graduates. You need to grow up and get a better head on your shoulders."

Eleanor's slap in the face stung for a long time, in part because I admired her savviness and sophistication. I took her critical words to heart. They not only wounded my already floundering sense of self, they also set me on a path of mistrust in her intentions toward me.

For some, criticism is a more natural part of life than affirming. The intent of our words and the way we communicate them determines whether they hurt or help. We are all critics, for better and worse, but we can gain mastery over what we say and how we say it. Being critical of others affects our psyche and brain as much as theirs. New neuroscience research reveals that criticism and other negative experiences actually lodge in our brains. By increasing the ratio of positives to negatives by five to one, we can tip the balance scale in our brain and our relationships to favor the positives. Understanding that criticism of others is rooted in self-judgment is a

step toward greater awareness. The way our criticism is interpreted is based on the foundation of our connection to the other person. Trust, respect, love, and care impact receptivity. We can transform our inner critic and build trust by developing an inner censor. As our inner climate changes we can learn to deliver purposeful criticism that helps, not hurts. With these insights we can even shift how we receive criticism ourselves.

Praise and Criticism

Affirming's natural associate is criticism. When I first started exploring the impact of criticism, I thought about hurtful words and negative labels, and recalled the judgmental comments a friend would replay from her long dead mother each time she looked in the mirror, "You're pretty, *but* you've got to lose weight..." I thought about parental criticisms—words of frustration, dispensed from a tired place at the end of a long day: "Can't you ever do your homework without someone sitting over you?" Or angry words that can't be taken back: "You always disappoint me."

My view of criticism was colored by the careless hurtful words I'd heard throughout my life. But as I thought more about praise and criticism, I realized how human it is to be judgmental; to view people, things, and experiences as either positive or negative. Words of praise or criticism result from these judgments. The problem with careless criticism is that it causes pain that can lodge forever in the hearts and minds of both receiver and giver.

Of course, criticism isn't always bad. When expressed with care and positive intent, it can help us grow and improve. Think about that a minute. How do we progress without feedback? When I began working on this book, I had a writing coach. I remember submitting to her the draft of my first chapter with the hope of feedback like, "You're an excellent writer. I love your ideas and your wording." Instead, she carefully said, "Okay. You've got your first thoughts on the page. Now you have to be less wordy." Though I felt crushed at first, I was grateful that her feedback gave me the direction and focus that enabled me to become a better writer.

Our Brains are Negativity Magnets

One television program I hate to miss is the newsmagazine show, *CBS Sunday Morning*. On the morning of the 2014 Academy Awards, Tracy Smith interviewed neuropsychologist Rick Hanson about the effects on nominees of movie critics' nasty comments. Hanson explained that the amygdala and the medial prefrontal cortex of the brain hold onto negative feelings and experiences much longer than positive ones. This reaction is rooted in our Stone Age brain—the part that stores recognized threats as a means of survival. Over the course of human evolution, bad experiences are hardwired to stick longer than we want them to, and good experiences have a tendency to roll off our backs and be forgotten. We remember painful experiences and hurtful words much longer than positive ones.

My stepmother, Eleanor, and I had a rough forty years together because each of our amygdala was loaded with negative experiences from one another. I triggered her as much as she triggered me. Whenever we'd visit, Eleanor's first words to me would often be complimentary, but things would quickly fall apart. If I disagreed with her or gave attention to my dad, Eleanor's emotions would disintegrate into a reactionary blow-up. "I *just* want a little of your time!" she'd shriek. "I don't know why I bother. You don't *care* about me. All you care about is your *daddy!*"

As her voice escalated, so did mine. "I was *just* talking with my dad for a few minutes. You and I spent the last hour looking at clothes! Can't I have a little time with each of you?" My body would become a board, my face steel, and my palpitating heart a closed door.

Each time we were together, I'd anticipate Eleanor's reactions. With an ever-growing negative bias, I'd become angry and resentful that again our precious family time was tainted by her emotional outbursts. She, in turn, held a negative bias toward me. She felt my judgments and could never accept being second place to my dad in my heart.

 Is there someone with whom you have a relationship that has an overload of negatives you'd like to shift? Write that person's name down and reflect on what causes the negative dynamic between you.

Five-to-One Ratio

The balance of negatives to positives makes all the difference in how a relationship feels. If there is more criticism and complaining than loving appreciation, our view of each other will end up being negative. As with Eleanor and me, a buildup of long-held judgments tipped the scale south.

Relationship psychologist John Gottman of the Gottman Institute confirms this balance from his research. After studying couples for decades, he found that marriages fell into the danger zone for divorce when the ratio of positive to negative interactions fell below five to one. This rule applies to all relationships, according to Gottman.

I'm so grateful I knew how to stream positive messages to my son as he was growing up. They counteracted the negative feedback he received from teachers who had difficulty seeing his capabilities masked by his ADHD. One particular instance of a teacher's blind criticism still pinches my heart. Theo loved history. His memory for information was like an elephant's, but he found his ninth grade history class dull and uninspiring. I said, "I'll bet honors history will have more stimulating discussions. Ask your teacher what you need to do to get into the honors class next year?"

He came back beaten and discouraged. "My teacher said, 'Forget it; you're not honors material. You don't even complete regular class work. You'd never be able to keep up.'" Then he added, "I guess honors history isn't for me, Mom."

We were both teary and I was outraged. There was no way I was going to leave my boy with those negative self-perceptions. So I said, "Unfortunately, your teacher doesn't stimulate your mind. She doesn't see your capabilities. Last year, Mr. Handel was blown away by your analysis of the causes of the Civil War. He raved about your ability to debate your point of view. And let's not forget your amazing memory for facts. You knew each battle, every general, and their connections to the politics of the time. You've got what it takes. It's just hard to stay motivated and excited when you don't feel engaged."

I was intent on showing Theo who he was, not who he wasn't.

Although the rest of the year was rough, with his persistence and my reinforcement, Theo eventually moved into honors and then Advanced Placement (AP) history. That success set his life on a personal and academic upswing. Counterbalancing the negatives with positives made the crucial difference.

The Root of Criticism–Self-Judgment

We all criticize and we all judge, whether we realize it or not. We judge others on their looks, behavior, the way they dress, their talents, mistakes, their successes and failures. Judging can be so much a part of our lives that it's sometimes hard to recognize when we're doing it.

I remember a stinging comment I flung at a friend in college. Val was a beauty queen type of girl. Her black shoulder length hair was carefully teased, flipped, and sprayed. Her face had layers of foundation, and her lashes were heavily mascaraed. While I was working on my fashionable, hippie look, she was dressed to the nines in tight skirts and heels. Val was sweet, vulnerable, and laughed easily. I was confused, insecure, and weathering my parents' separation with my flimsy sense of self.

As we sat on her dorm room bed, I blurted, "Why do you wear so much makeup and all those fancy clothes? You look so fake. If you really want people to like you, you should just be yourself." I can still see tears staining her cheeks, and feel piercing shame for transferring my own feelings of fakeness onto her. I was the one who was inauthentic, trying so hard to fit in.

The truth about our judgments of others is that they're often rooted in our own self-judgment. We tear apart people who are doing better than we are, and get strength from people who are doing worse. We judge our own success against others'. Some we judge are role models we aspire to be like, while others might exude an egoist confidence we despise. Who are they to be so beautiful, lucky, and proud, while we aren't?

There was one such woman I recall from Theo's Little League days. Brittany had obviously been a cheerleader in high school. She was blonde, beautiful, and had lungs loud enough to be heard on the next playing field. She also exuded confidence that was to die for. Her son Bill was the pitcher and was equally powerful in confidence and skill. Brittany would stand on the metal bleachers at dusk with hands cupped around her mouth screaming, "Come on, Bill, get 'im out! You've got it Blue Jays; it's in the bag!"

I remember saying to Gus, "Brittany has such a big mouth. She acts like she owns the place and always makes sure Bill gets top billing. I can't stand her."

I was jealous. I hadn't been a cheerleader, and the whole sports scene was new to me. She had a comfort level

I yearned for. Looking back now, I understand that Brittany was in her element supporting her son and the team. My judgments reflected my insecurities.

When we suspend judgment, we can learn a lot. There was a time I looked with judgment upon people who were homeless. Then I encountered the beautiful soul of a woman who had lost her home.

I was suffering deeply due to the illness of a family member and was on the phone with a travel insurance representative, trying to recover our plane fare from a cancelled trip. Rita, on the other end of the line in Guatemala, spoke to me with a level of kindness and compassion that moved me to tears.

"I understand your pain," she said. "Six months ago I lost my husband and our house. I was homeless. Now I live with my parents and get to take care of them at the end of their lives. You'll see. God will take care of you."

As Rita shared her story I understood the dire circumstances that led her to homelessness. Our brief encounter made me think about homelessness in a new light. It made me recognize that suffering and loss are human emotions we all share.

Now I look for commonalities, rather than cutting people out with judgmental thoughts. Acceptance helps us feel more connected to others and to ourselves—another gift of living the affirming way of life.

Nurture Your Inner Censor— Will My Words Help or Hurt?

Judging ourselves, judging others, saying whatever comes to mind without censoring—how do we break that cycle? "Start by being mindful," says Jon Kabat-Zinn, author, professor emeritus of medicine at the University of Massachusetts, and father of the mindfulness movement.

Kabat-Zinn defines mindfulness as paying attention, on purpose, in the present moment, nonjudgmentally. We can develop the habit of mindfulness in regards to our critical words by noticing our judgmental thoughts and catching ourselves before acting on them.

If I speak impulsively, as I tend to do with those closest to me, it's going to blow up in my face, causing them and me, more harm than good. My sister, Lois, tells me she wants to fit into the rose-colored dress she wore to her daughter's wedding for our nephew's upcoming marriage. I'm about to blurt out, "Then don't eat sweets at night and exercise more," but I mentally cup my hand over my mouth and keep quiet. Instead, I ask myself, *Will this advice help or hurt?* Then I know my answer.

I remember other times when I've advised my sister on weight loss, her response was, "You don't have any idea how hard it is to lose weight! You're skinny. You do it your way, and I'll do it mine." Now, instead of advising, I ask, "How are you doing with the dieting?" She tells me her plan and I encourage her by saying, "You've lost the weight before and you can do it again." She's not looking for advice— she's looking for support.

Again and again I mindfully, mentally clamp my hand over my mouth to catch myself before saying something unnecessary or undermining. Gus is wearing a brown jacket with black pants and a red checkered shirt as he leaves for work. The combination looks bad to me. I'm about to blurt, "That doesn't go…," but I stop and think, *Does it really matter?* He's not having an important meeting today, and he's nearly out the door. Instead I say, "Have a great day, honey."

So many things that I used to consider important, I find really aren't. My friend cancels our day at the beach; my cousin is fifteen minutes late for lunch; my neighbor's son has a party with music booming into the early morning hours. In the past I would have commented judgmentally about these minor things; now I say to myself, *So what?* I realize if I say what I'm thinking, my careless words will hurt my relationships more than help.

At the same time, I know that when I am asked for advice, my honesty matters, but my words need not sting. My friend Myra calls and tells me her stepdaughter is asking to borrow a thousand dollars. Myra's husband wants to lend it to her, but Myra is dead set against it. "What do you think?" she asks. I think Myra's not seeing the larger picture, and might do well to consider her husband's point of view. I respond, "How do you think Sam would feel if he didn't lend her the money? If it's that important to him, I think you should do it."

I hear an audible sigh. "You're right. I didn't think she deserved it, but Sam's feelings are more important. I knew I could count on you to help me see the bigger picture."

When I'm about to react or judge, I pause and put myself in the other person's shoes to help me notice that I too have made similar mistakes. Driving is a wonderful metaphor for accepting others' imperfections. If someone cuts me off, I give them slack because I've cut others off too. If an older person drives slowly, I recall that I have a tendency to drive slowly when I'm talking to my passenger. When I see a crazy speeding driver, as long as I am safely out of their path, I remind myself I too have sped when running late.

Feeling my connection to all people as humans with strengths and weaknesses, who love their families and want to be loved, who have goals and dreams, just like me, helps me to mindfully censor my judgmental self.

 Is there a person or situation you tend to be judgmental with? Consider how you might handle it differently. Jot some ideas in your notebook.

Purposeful Criticism

My sister was getting married amidst the messiest time of our parents' divorce. Aunt Lil, my mother's sister and protector, was beyond livid with my father for leaving my vulnerable, needy mother. She was determined that Dad would not feel honored at the wedding.

"Are you crazy?" Aunt Lil said to Lois. "You want to invite your father's sister Sarah and her sons so your father can feel proud in front of them? You know he didn't just leave your mother... he left you girls too. He's not helping with the wedding in any way and he doesn't care about your feelings. Don't be stupid! Let him feel pushed to the side, just like he's done with you! Where are your smarts?"

Aunt Lil's words made Lois a nervous wreck, my mother weepy, and me seethe with anger. Her words stung because they actually mirrored the way we felt. We didn't need her to rub it in.

Always the peacemaker, Uncle Marty, Aunt Lil's husband, grabbed the phone. "Your aunt has only the best intentions. She loves your mother and you girls and this is her way of showing it."

Forty years later I finally get this, but at the time Aunt Lil caused my mother, my sister, and me great pain and turmoil. In an effort to protect us, she neglected to consider the impact of her critical words.

All of our words have an effect on others, often much greater than we fathom. The lesson I learned from Aunt Lil was the importance of considering the potential impact of the words we say.

Purposeful criticism, in contrast to hurtful criticism, is given with compassion, and the conscious intent of supporting the other person's growth, inner strength, or the relationship we share with them. Sometimes we can be so focused on our own hurts or expectations that we don't put ourselves in the other person's shoes. In purposeful criticism, we consider the other person's feelings, reactions, needs, and goals right alongside our own.

Stepping into the other person's shoes changes our feedback. If we focus on their strengths and positive qualities, we view the other person with respect and treat them with dignity whether or not we agree with their actions. Respect and heartfelt appreciation for the people in our lives creates *a foundation of trust* from which we can give purposeful criticism.

Janet, my fifth-grade, bilingual co-teacher, was a young woman new to teaching. She had a side-splitting sense of humor, and her jokey, warm personality made me laugh and smile every day. The problem was, she didn't seem to draw the line when it came to joking freely with our students.

"I don't get it. The kids seem to respect you so much more than me," she said. "It's like you're the teacher and I'm their friend. What am I doing wrong?"

My first thought was, *I want to be honest with Janet about her teaching style while helping her have faith in her ability to command respect.*

"I think the difference is that I use my serious demeanor to let them know I have serious expectations of them. It's only when I see them taking our class rules seriously that I loosen up. Try thinking, *I am in charge here* and take charge with your voice and expectations. Look how you created such effective reading lesson plans. You work hard and you're determined to be an excellent teacher. I know you're going to master this too."

Janet trusted me enough to share with me her sense of inadequacy. I followed up my advice to her with encouraging words that I told her often. My purpose was to leave her knowing she had what it took to be the authority in the classroom, which is eventually what happened.

It's harder to give purposeful criticism when trust isn't established. Relationships aren't automatically grounded on trust. Trust is built over time with the sharing of feelings and experiences. If we come from a place of respect, compassion, and clarity, the way we deliver our feedback can help us accomplish our purpose and foster growth.

Here are some tips on how to apply purposeful criticism from a leadership position where trust isn't a given.

- *Get your emotions in check first, before delivering the feedback* – we can feel a whole range of negative feelings in regards to someone's behavior and their impact on a project. Deal with your reactions first, so you can come from a neutral no-blaming place.

- *Set your mind on their capability* – before you speak to your employee or team member, focus your thoughts on the qualities you respect and appreciate in them. When we see the best in people, we act from the best in ourselves.

- *Use descriptive, nonjudgmental language* – "I notice you've been arriving late and leaving early. Is everything ok?"

- *Be specific about your expectations, then ask a question, brainstorm solutions together, or offer a suggestion* – "Your data is necessary for us to get our new website up and running. We need it in two weeks. What seems to be getting in the way of completing it? You might try…"

- *Recognize their potential contribution* – "You are so thorough in the way you gather and compile data. We really value your skills."

Consider the Receiver's Experience Level in Delivering Purposeful Criticism

With or without a foundation of trust, the receiver's experience level is an important factor to consider when offering feedback. Business professors Stacey Finkelstein and Ayelet Fishbach, in their *Journal of Consumer Research* article, "Tell Me What I Did Wrong: Experts Seek and Respond to Negative Feedback," found that people seek and benefit from different types of feedback based on their level of experience. Novices who are just starting out are looking for encouragement, while people with a base of experience or expertise want specific feedback on how they can improve.

The judges on *Dancing with the Stars* beautifully demonstrate the art of giving criticism based on a contestant's confidence and skill level. Gus and I loyally watch the show every season. Twelve celebrities from backgrounds other than dancing, pair up with professional dancers to compete for the Mirrorball trophy. The three judges are charged with giving purposeful criticism after each dance to help the contestants improve. Though their comments can at times be sarcastic and could use some censoring, I've observed differences in feedback based on the contestant's experience and confidence level.

During Season 23, Terra Jole, a star on the television series, *Little Women,* exhibited a tender yet determined spirit. She tearfully expressed how she wanted to be judged as a person, not a little person. After her first dance with her partner, Sasha, Judge Carrie Ann Inaba said, "I didn't see a little person; I saw a huge star—a sexy, sultry person, every kick and turn in the right place. Well done!" Terra beamed. Judge Carrie Ann's words seemed to lift Terra sky high. She was a novice with obvious grace who needed encouragement to bolster her confidence on the dance floor.

James Hinchcliffe, an award-winning IndyCar racer, showed a stronger base of assets from the start. The criticism he received was more specific. After dancing a Pasa Doble in week two with his partner Sharna, Judge Carrie Ann said, "Impressive synchronicity! However, this week was not as strong as last week's performance. Too vertical. Just think of your arms as stretching out." Her criticism was specifically aimed to help him get better.

Even when the person is experienced and eager to get purposeful criticism, encouragement always heightens their hopes. Erin Andrews, one of the show's co-hosts, picked up cues on the effect of Carrie Ann's feedback from James's downturned mouth. "You probably were looking for reassurance. You received those comments because the judges know you can handle it. You're already so great; they know you can grow. You're crushing it on the racetrack and the dance floor."

Dealing with Criticism

As long as we are alive and interacting with others in the world, we can expect to be criticized. We all have been. Criticism can sometimes have a crushing effect that can cause us to doubt ourselves for an extended period of time. As I mentioned before, this was the case with my stepmother because her criticisms fed into my feelings of inadequacy.

Thankfully, I came across a pivotal idea years ago that helped me more effectively handle criticism: "Don't take anything personally." In his book *The Four Agreements* Don Miguel Ruiz offers this wise advice, and it really works.

He explains that whatever people say to us is colored by *their* mindset, *their* life experiences, and *their* feelings about themselves. This idea was a revelation to me. It helped me step back when I was feeling insulted and ask myself, *"Where is this criticism coming from? How does it reflect the person giving it?"*

When my stepmother was in her late eighties, she developed Parkinson's. She needed help dressing, getting into the car, and managing most tasks using her hands or requiring balance. Although an undercurrent of mistrust still existed between us, my heart went out to Eleanor seeing this active, independent woman become extremely dependent. I was happy to focus on whatever she needed when we were together. At the end of one particular visit, when I'd been assisting her all day, I said, "Why don't I help you put on this pretty, flowered nightgown?"

"You are *so* controlling!" she screamed. "*I'm* in charge of me!"

I was livid and hurt, but when I thought about it later, I said to myself, *Eleanor feels out of control. Her words are about her need for control. But is there also some truth in what she said? Am I controlling?*

Stepping back to reflect on both the criticizer's point of view, and the truth in their words, is the gift of being criticized. Eleanor frequently spoke of others being controlling, even before her illness, so I knew that was her issue. But maybe I wasn't being empathic enough. Perhaps my suggestion made Eleanor feel diminished—a reminder that she wasn't even in control of dressing herself. Her criticism became a growth opportunity for me.

If we are hurt by someone's words, it can be a signal that deep down we believe their words are true.

I remember when I first married Gus, we were at a friend's wedding and I wanted to impress him with my appeal. As we chatted with Brian, a handsome man I worked with, I laughed brightly, gave Brian a warm hug, and exuded an overall sexy energy. When we were alone, Gus coldly said, "You're a flirt. You embarrassed me when you cozied up to Brian. If that's how you're going to act, don't expect me to go to any of your work events."

I was crushed. I felt such shame. While I thought Gus would see me as more irresistable, my actions actually had the opposite effect. His words stung because they were true. I had been a flirt my whole life. Gus's criticism was a valuable lesson for me to clean up my foolish behavior because his feelings were what mattered most.

In her 99u talk, "Why Your Critics Aren't the Ones Who Count" (2013), Brené Brown says, "If you are bold enough to put your work into the world, be prepared for backlash." She described what happened after her 2010 TED talk, "The Power of Vulnerability," went viral. Although she was warned not to read the online comments about her, she couldn't resist. She said the criticisms were mean personal attacks. People said things like, "Of course she embraces imperfection, look at how she looks," and "Less research, more Botox."

After eight hours immobilized lying on her couch watching TV, she remembered a Theodore Roosevelt quote, which put everything in perspective for her:

"It is not the critic who counts; not the man who points out how the strong man stumbles...the credit belongs to the man who is actually in the arena...who strives valiantly; who errs, who comes short again and again, because there is no effort without error and shortcoming..."

Brown says successful people take risks. Instead of shying away from the critics, expect them to be seated in the front row seats, be prepared for what they will say, and ignore them. "Say, 'I hear you, but I'll do this anyway.'"

 How do you deal with criticism? Do you take it personally? Do you consider where the other person is coming from? You might want to journal about this.

Is there a behavior someone has called you out on that may have some truth to it? Can you take responsibility for your behavior and embrace it as an opportunity to grow?

Give What You Want

Recently through Facebook I had the joy of being reunited with my favorite childhood neighbor. Roberta and I hadn't spoken to one another since we were ten. As we walked through the park catching up on each other's lives, she said something so wise. "I used to have expectations of people and I'd be disappointed. Now I just give what I want to receive. If I want to see a friend who hasn't called, I call her. If I'm waiting for my brother and his wife to reciprocate an invitation, I invite them. I'm much happier living this way."

I think Roberta's approach is brilliant. I can see the peace and pleasure it gives her, and it connects so beautifully to living the affirming way of life. Give to others what you want. Give acceptance rather than judgment. Cut others slack, rather than jumping to find fault. Look with eyes that see the best in others, rather than the worst. Accept imperfection. Soften your criticisms, and make your life, and the lives of those near and dear, sweeter.

Your Takeaways

1. **Consider, "Will my words or advice help or hurt?"**

2. **Clamp that imaginary hand over your mouth to censor hurtful words.**

3. **Live by the five-to-one ratio, five affirmations to every criticism.**

4. Become observant of your judgmental thoughts. Know it's human to judge, but consider judgments as opportunities to choose to see more of the good in other people.

5. Ask these experience level questions: "Is this person a novice?" Then give encouragement. "Is this person experienced?" Then encourage with specific direction on how to improve.

6. Don't take criticism personally. Ask yourself, "Where is this criticism coming from? How does it reflect the person giving it?"

7. When criticized, reflect on the truth in the other person's words (if there is any) and embrace it as a growth opportunity.

8. Give what you want to receive—acceptance, slack for being human, eyes that see the best in others.

PART TWO

The Forms of Affirming

CHAPTER 4

Self-Supporting Words

I was sitting with my grown niece, Mary Jo, on her mother's soft floral couch watching a Greek TV soap opera. Mary Jo was laughing and shaking her head in agreement with the attractive woman speaking emotionally on the screen.

"What's so funny?" I asked, as my understanding of the Greek language is minimal. Mary Jo proceeded to translate the scene for me:

"This woman is sleeping at her boyfriend's house, gets up in the middle of the night, and walks down the hall to the kitchen. Her boyfriend hears her saying to someone, "I love you. You're smart and so good-looking. You make me so happy. You're a treasure. I'm so thankful for you."

When she comes back to the bedroom, he angrily yells, "Ok. Who is he? I know you're cheating on me because I heard every word you said to that bastard!"

"Hah!" she shouts. "Asynetos! (Stupid!) I was just saying to myself all the things I wish you would say to me!"

That character in the Greek comedy knew something that benefits us all—the affirming way of life begins with what's inside us. Our positive words for others are founded on our positive words for ourselves. Most of us, though, have loud inner critical voices to reckon with. Recognizing our inner critic is a first step in transforming it. We can begin to find positive words for ourselves by mimicking the voice of someone who speaks to us lovingly and supportively. There are so many small daily opportunities to do this. When our inner critic raises its head, as it will, try holding up an imaginary sign that says, "STOP DON'T GO THERE." Let that critical voice know it isn't welcome. Create personal affirmations—positive self-statements mentally repeated over and over to saturate our psyche with all the goodness we possess.

Positive Words for You

So far, living the affirming way of life has been about developing a greater capacity to notice the good in others and to generously tell them. But where do those positive feelings spring from? They come from *you*. The bedrock of the affirming way of life is your relationship with yourself.

Buddhist meditation teacher Jack Kornfield explains, "We begin with loving our self because without loving our self it's almost impossible to love others." If we don't have loving affirming words for ourselves, how can we muster them for anyone else? I'm not saying it's easy to speak lovingly to your own self, especially if your inner voice is critical. But if you want positive relationships with others, it's essential to first show compassion toward yourself.

During my middle years of teaching and parenting, I constantly knocked myself over the head with an internal verbal club. My inner critic harped at me about nearly everything I did. *You didn't teach that lesson well. The team resents you for always being late. Theo keeps getting in trouble at school because you're not a good parent. You're doing everything wrong.* There was no end to the negative messages I fed myself.

Dealing with the reactions of Theo's teachers to his ADHD, threw me back to the years growing up in the wake of my mother's bipolar disorder. My childhood shame resurfaced, and I felt disconnected from others. Over time, that changed, as I learned to speak kindly and lovingly to myself. But how do we get to that place?

The Inner Critic

For any of us with inner critical voices, put-downs can become so much a part of us that we become unable to separate our essence from the negative things we tell ourselves. Our inner voice may sound something like the voice of Cinderella's evil stepmother screeching in our ears, "You lazy good for nothing! You call that chimney swept? You're worthless! No one would ever want you." Over time we in-ternalize that negative voice as our own. Even though Cin-derella was a kind and loving person, she sadly absorbed a sense of worthlessness from the critical messages she was given. Many of us have done the same thing by internaliz-ing negative voices from our formative years.

Understanding where the mean-spirited voice comes from, and the fact that it's erroneous, can help us begin to separate our healthy sense of self from our hurtful inner critic.

In her book *Self-Compassion,* Kristin Neff confirms that for many of us, the critical voice stems from being criticized as children. Often our parents criticized us in an effort to keep us safe from trouble or to motivate us to work harder. Maybe our parents were raised with a lot of negative talk themselves and were unconsciously repeating the pattern. Maybe they were unaware of the negative affect criticism had on them, and in turn on their own children.

I think of my friend Brandi, a beautiful woman inside and out. She has a strong marriage, three great kids, gath-ers friends and family at her gracious home, and runs a successful party planning business. Yet Brandi tells me that when she has to give a presentation to clients her heart palpitates and her hands sweat because she hears in her head the words her father said throughout her childhood: "Speak up! Are you a mouse? No one's going to listen to you if you mumble." She can't seem to shake her father's critical voice.

Neff says the criticism we turn on ourselves can come from any influential person in our childhood—a grandpar-ent, sibling, teacher, or even a coach. Jon, a friend who is over forty and still looking for his Ms. Right, said all through his years growing up his older sister would say, "You're such a nerd with your glasses and skinny body, you'll never get a girl. You read all the time, you're so boring." Even though Jon has a successful career, he can't shake the image of himself as a guy no woman would want.

Our critical voice may also be rooted in perfectionism. Brené Brown, in her enlightening book *The Gift of Imperfection* explains that we adapt a perfectionist mentality to avoid criticism. Perfectionists believe that if they look, act, and live perfectly, they can protect themselves from being judged and feeling their underlying shame. The perfectionist mindset may come from having a parent with high expectations who we never seem to satisfy. It can also result from covering the shame that develops when we come from a family with challenges like alcoholism, mental illness, or physical disabilities.

Growing up, I had a double whammy that lead to the perfectionist curse. In the depression phase of my mother's illness, she had no sense of order. Our house was messy, dirty, and made me feel deeply ashamed. The shame intensified when I'd visit my neighbor Roberta whose house was immaculate, right down to the specially-sized plastic containers that held her family's spaghetti and cereal. When my mother was in her manic phase, she'd humiliate me by complaining about my father to everyone she could find, from the bank teller to my teachers.

My dad was a striver for self-improvement and increasing his standing in the world. His perfectionist self would never leave the house until his shoes were shined, his face closely-shaven, and his pants crisply ironed. To relax when he was in college, my dad would read his chemistry books. Enough said! He expected me to earn straight A's. When I'd show him my report card, his focus went straight to the B's. I felt like a disappointment. I tried to impress my dad by behaving like him—speaking intelligently and reading avidly, but I never felt I made the grade.

The problem with the perfectionist mentality is that it makes us work at projecting to others that we have it all together, while inside we feel shame for not living up to impossible expectations.

Neff's second core component of self-compassion is a life-changer. She calls it "recognition of our common humanity." By this she means that a big part of being human is to make mistakes, suffer, and feel inadequate—not just us, but everyone. It helps to understand that countless people have critical voices in their heads. If we can remember we're not that voice, we can begin to change it.

 Do you have a critical inner sound track demanding perfection of yourself? Take a closer look by jotting down what your voice says and where you think that message may have come from. Then ask yourself if what that voice says really applies to you, or is it something to toss away!

Develop a New Voice

My own transition from the negative voice to a supportive one developed as the result of a major life change. I was in my thirties and drowning in a ten-year relationship with a loving man I knew I would never marry. James had been my ideal father-substitute after my parent's divorce. I was the center of his universe. He lavished me with compliments and made me feel secure when my father cut me off emotionally after his marriage to Eleanor. The problem was, James and I were miles apart in our values and goals.

When I finally found the courage to leave James, I had to face the void. I'd awaken in the morning with a feeling of emptiness that would quickly be filled with self-recrimination. *You used him. You deserve to be alone. You're a terrible person! You'll probably never meet anyone else.*

One morning I awoke with a brainstorm. I said to myself, *Pretend you're James. What would he say?* I rolled over in bed, hugged myself the way James would have, and said aloud, "I love you, Gailie. You're wonderful. I'm so proud of you." These words, which were his words, made me feel supported and strong. That was the start of my self-supporting voice. Though they sounded unreal at first, I repeated those loving words every morning before I got out of bed, and before long they started working.

Even now, self-supporting words help me start each day from a positive place. This practice has extended over time to become encouraging words I say to myself when I'm disappointed with something I've done. *It's ok. You made a mistake. You'll do better next time.* I speak to myself with the kindness and compassion that I would give to anyone else. This frees me from the heavy weight of my own put-downs.

I gather supportive words like collectors gather art. When I separated from James, although my loving morning ritual helped me start my day in a better place, as the day wore on my positive thinking reserves often became bone dry. So I sought new supportive voices to replenish me in the form of two dear older and wiser friends. Ann, a teaching teammate, would listen compassionately to my fears and worries, and after all was said, Ann would declare in the most compassionate voice, "It'll be fine." In the late afternoon when I returned home, Irv, a farmer-mechanic neighbor, listened to my fears and doubts as we walked through his vegetable garden plucking Japanese beetles off his potato plants. "You're going to make it," he repeated reassuringly. I became attuned to the comfort these two lovingly-offered phrases brought. In time I was able to say them to myself and even give them away to others.

During that difficult period of my life, I often listened to Louise Hay's affirmation tapes as I drove to work. Hay is best known for her emotionally healing book *You Can Heal Your Life*. On her tapes she recites positive, mind-shifting statements for the listener to repeat such as, "I approve of myself." I would then say those words right along with her. Over time, choosing to repeat positive phrases helped me anchor my self-supporting, inner voice. To this day whenever people compliment me I repeat their words in my head when I'm alone. When my sister says, "I always admire how strong and determined you are," I say her words to myself, remembering how these words once felt like the furthest thing from the truth. When my dear friend Lynn says, "You are the only person I trust to give me honest feedback from a larger perspective," I reiterate her words in my mind, savoring their message.

Repeating the positive words others say to you, slowly and surely further opens your heart to yourself. And once your heart is open, you will discover that the most important affirmer in your life is you.

Become Your Own Fan

In the first chapter, I told a story about how the superintendent of schools in our town left a legacy of confidence to his sons because they could count on him to be their fan. Well, once I replaced Cinderella's stepmother's voice with my supportive one, I became my own biggest fan. It's so important for all of us to do this because we are our most constant companions.

When I invoke loving, confidence-boosting words for myself, it's often in response to negative voices that still manage to show up. My perfectionist internal dad can still give me a hard time when I make mistakes. Recently, some friends took me out for a lovely birthday lunch. Toward the end of the meal, I ordered a dinner to take home for Gus. When I paid the bill with my credit card, I didn't leave a tip because my friends said they'd tipped generously. The waiter, who had been so kind and responsive, returned with Gus's dinner with a scowl on his face which I could only infer was because he felt I had been cheap with him. I felt terrible that I hadn't shown appreciation for his kindness. When I got in my car to leave, I lamented my mistake, but my self-supportive voice stepped up. *It's OK,* I said to myself. *You're not comfortable with the choice you made. You can see it's important to you to be considerate. Next time you won't make this mistake. It'll be fine.* I speak to myself in a compassionate voice that sounds like my friend Ann's, and after a short while I am able to let the mistake go and be present-focused again. Reassuring words are something I need daily. I can count on me to give them.

The helpless voice of my mother still has me approach certain tasks and goals as if I'm climbing Mt. Everest. In my head she says things like, *This is hard. I don't know how you'll do it.* But now, as my own fan, I keep on trekking, thanks to self-supporting words of pride and encouragement.

The power of being self-supportive still amazes me. Recently I had a new student to tutor in writing. I had trepidation because he's in sixth grade, beyond the grade I taught. I was unsure whether the approach I was planning to take would give him the tools he needed to do the writing assignment from his teacher.

After we talked a little, he revealed he had difficulty organizing his ideas. I said, "Hey, Colin, I'm a writer myself. Come into my writing room and I'll show you how I do it." I tell him how I, too, needed a tutor—a writing coach—and showed him the brainstorms, outlines, and revisions for the chapter I was working on.

Colin was impressed by what he called my pre-planning work, and by the time his mom came to pick him up we were both pleased with his progress. After the two left, I joyfully applauded myself: *You found the just right way to help Colin organize his ideas, and you used the time so well that he was able to complete the essay. I'm proud of you!* I spoke with specific, enthusiastic praise just like I would to strengthen another person. My words turned what started as an insecure experience into a joyful one.

It's comforting and enlightening to realize that within ourselves we have available love, support, and wisdom when we need them most. Affirming words from others are gravy, but self-supporting words are the main course.

 What self-supporting words do you want or need to hear?

Start with "I'm proud of you..." Jot others that come to you in your notebook. Whatever comes up is exactly what you need. Embrace your new words and make them a part of your inner being.

Stop! Don't Go There

You may develop a kinder more self-supportive internal voice, but that doesn't mean Cinderella's stepmother will never rear her critical head. Thoughts that go against your more positive stand in life will still come knocking at your door, but you can learn how to ignore them.

I used to be plagued by the curse of comparing myself to others. If someone's house was nicer, their children were doing better, or their job was more prestigious, my step-mother's voice would say, *You're not as good.*

One evening while driving home together from a po-etry festival, my friend Nancy turned to me and asked, "How's Theo doing?"

"Oh, he's fine, but I wish I'd been smart and gotten him private baseball coaching lessons like my neighbor gave her son."

"Why is that necessary?" she asked.

"Theo loves baseball, but he gets overlooked on his Lit-tle League team because his skills are average, while my neighbor's son is a star."

"You've always done what you believe is best for Theo. Maybe he's happy where he is. That comparing thing is un-healthy, sweetie." I knew her words were true and we talked about what I could do to break the pattern. On the spot an image came to her. "Whenever you start comparing your-self to others, imagine raising a big red stop sign and say-ing to yourself, 'STOP! DON'T GO THERE!' If you catch yourself each moment your comparing voice rears its head, I bet you can put that counterproductive habit to rest."

That was over ten years ago. Now the phrase has be-come a trusted friend. I rarely compare anymore, but if I become absorbed in thoughts which I recognize as mental pollution (like dredging up old grievances or judging) I raise that stop sign in my mind and command myself under my breath, "NO. STOP! DON'T GO THERE!"

Try keeping your Cinderella's stepmother's voice away by posting a guard with a trusty stop sign whenever critical words arise. Each moment you fend off unproductive inner dialogue, you strengthen the positive voice you choose.

Affirmations of Another Kind

The final piece to making your inner voice totally self-sup-portive is saturating your mind with affirmations—positive statements repeated regularly until they become your reality.

After I left my long-time boyfriend, James, my friend Nancy and I became single-woman buddies. We helped each other develop affirmations to fuel our belief in meet-ing our just-right men. One of my affirmations was, "I have met my just-right man, and I am happier than I ever dreamed possible." Every time I'd get in my car, I'd recite my affirmations aloud with feeling, as though they were to-tally true and I was enjoying the benefits. And you know what? Over time the intention behind the affirmations be-came my reality. I *did* meet my just-right man, I *am* happier than I ever dreamed was possible, and we've been married for twenty-nine years as I write this book.

I'm not saying that affirmations are guaranteed to work every time, but they can lift you out of negative thinking patterns, help you feel more hopeful, and prime you to take actions that help make your vision a reality. In his article "Brain Scans Can Help Explain Why Self-Affir-mation Works," Christian Jarrett cites exciting evidence from the research of neuropsychologist Christopher Cas-cio and colleagues at the University of Pennsylvania that affirmations stimulate activity in brain centers and can even affect our actions. They found that participants had greater activation in the ventral striatum and the ventral medial prefrontal cortex, parts of the brain known to be involved in expecting and receiving rewards. The researchers found the future-oriented aspect of affirmations was what specifically impacted brain activity. And the most surprising discovery was the way affirmations affected the participants' lives. Those who created an affirmation to become more active actually did.

Many successful people use affirmations to create what they want in life. Suze Orman, the financial guru, author, and TV host, said she began her quest to acquire wealth by saying daily, "I have more money than I will ever need." Boxing great Muhammad Ali said he repeated, "I am the greatest," before he ever believed it. Jim Carrey, Will Smith, Lady Gaga, and so many other successful people attribute the use of affirmations to creating the positive mindset that helped them achieve their goals.

Creating and using affirmations is consciously choosing to immerse your mind in positive thoughts in order to shape your reality. Here are some guidelines to create your own affirmations.

- Start with the words, "I am." The subconscious mind interprets those words as a command to make what they say happen.

- Word your affirmation as if it's already a reality. "I am happily working at my dream job."

- Use positive statements only. Avoid saying, "I will not...," or, "I don't..." The subconscious does not recognize the word no. If you say, "I will *not* eat sweets," the subconscious hears, "I will eat sweets."

- Include at least one action verb; it adds dynamism to your affirmation. "I easily *run* a half-marathon."
- Include one emotion word to interject the joy of the fulfillment of your goal. "I am *happier* than I ever dreamed possible with my just-right mate."

Brandi, the woman who chanted her father's critical words every time she had to speak to a group, could create an affirmation to help herself feel confident making presentations. It might sound something like this: "I am relaxed and confident making presentations. Whatever I say is well received and I feel *spectacular*."

Jon, my single friend who'd love to have a life partner, might create an affirmation that says, "I confidently approach women who are *very* attracted to me."

Affirmations are a staple of my life, as much a part of my daily routine as eating, brushing my teeth, or exercising.

You are the voice you listen to the most each day. Build the self-supportive habit by speaking lovingly to yourself. Stop negative self-talk in its tracks, and saturate your thoughts with affirmations of the person you are just on the brink of becoming.

Your Takeaways...

1. Speak lovingly, proudly, kindly, and compassionately to yourself. Give yourself the words you wish someone else would say to you.

2. Embrace your imperfections as part of being human.

3. Notice your critical inner voice when it rears its head, and say "STOP! DON'T GO THERE!" to silence it, then replace it with a kinder message.

4. Create affirmations—statements about something you want to be or have, as if they are already true. Repeat your affirmations daily and as often as possible to immerse your thoughts in the reality you desire.

CHAPTER 5

Recognition Words

I graduated from Syracuse University with a major in child development and had no idea of what to do next. My sister, three years younger and only a freshman in college, gave me much-needed direction.

"When I visited you at college and saw you working with preschoolers, it was magical. You just lit up. You were patient, and you instinctively understood how to talk to the kids on their level. They seemed to love you. I think you're a natural teacher."

I had never considered teaching as a career, but Lois made me realize how alive I felt in the classroom. My sister's prompting gave me a direction to explore. I so enjoyed teaching preschoolers that I got a master's in education and ended up nurturing the minds and spirits of children for thirty-eight years. By describing to me the talents she'd observed, Lois opened my mind and my life to greater possibility. This is the gift of words of recognition.

Recognition words are a deeper form of affirming. Often, our capabilities may remain invisible to our mind's eye until someone else recognizes them and tells us. Recognition words can help us identify and accept our greater potentials and positive qualities. Research reveals that we can benefit from "mirrors" held up by others, which reinforce our capabilities. Recognition words can confirm we're on the right path, build our confidence, and help support a positive life change. As we attune our mind to repeated recognition, hearing can become believing. We can then become self-supporting and recognize our own magnificent qualities. Don't hold back when you notice wonderful qualities in others. Your positive words really do matter! Giving and receiving recognition can have a positive influence beyond what you've ever imagined.

The Invisible Made Visible

A wonderful example of the gift of recognition was in an episode of the PBS TV series, *Downton Abbey*. Daisy, the twenty-year-old assistant cook at Downton, was unsatisfied with her work and wanted to do more with her life. She ordered mathematics books, but as she began studying, self-doubt reared its nasty head.

"I'm thick. I just can't learn," she lamented to Mrs. Patmore, the head cook.

"Certainly you can. Maybe you just need some tutoring. Why not ask Miss Bunting to help you?"

So Daisy solicited Miss Bunting, the village teacher, to tutor her in math. After two sessions of working together, Miss Bunting declared, "Daisy, you're quick and smart. You'll get the hang of numbers in no time."

Miss Bunting's words of recognition were life-changing for Daisy. Whenever she wasn't working in the kitchen, her head was craned over her books doing problems and excitedly talking to the other staff about her future plans.

"When I finish my studies, I'm going to do accounting," she'd proudly declare.

Recognition means:

1. to accept or be aware that something is true or exists.

2. to accept as official.

3. to identify.

Recognition words from Miss Bunting boosted Daisy's confidence and self-worth as she became aware of her own competencies and accepted that the perceptions of her trusted teacher were true and official. Quick and smart became Daisy's new identity.

Recognition words are a deeper form of affirming that can help us accept as true some previously unknown parts of ourselves.

Mirrors

Positive psychology is a field that examines how ordinary people can become happier and more fulfilled. It offers evidence that supports living the affirming way of life. In a *Sage Journal* article, "Others Sometimes Know Us Better Than We Know Ourselves," positive psychologists Simine Vazine and Erika Carlson substantiate that we often rely on trusted others to reveal to us unknown parts of ourselves. Vazine and Carlson explain that although we may know our internal feelings, we may still have blind spots—aspects of ourselves we just don't see. Those who know us can sometimes see strengths in us that we may not see ourselves. When Theo was young, Gus and I noticed that he was a riveting speaker and frequently told him so. As he grew up, Theo loved making presentations and, while in college, even had the honor of giving a TEDx talk. (TED stands for Technology, Entertainment, and Design, and is a nonprofit dedicated to spreading ideas in the form of short, powerful talks.)

Recognition words can be like a mirror. We go through our days, doing what we do, until someone generously reflects back in words something special they see in us. Then we begin to see it, too.

My friend Jamie Sussel Turner, author of *Less Stress Business*, told me a story about how a principal's recognition of her leadership ability propelled her career. "As a young teacher it never occurred to me to go to graduate school. No one in my family had. My principal Mary Lee Fitzgerald encouraged me to begin graduate studies. She wrote in my evaluation, 'Jamie, you have a great deal to contribute to the teaching profession, and perhaps, public education in general. At this point of the year, my evaluation of your performance places you at the top of the staff for sheer professional excellence.' Mary Lee's words helped me to see my potential as an educational leader. I went on to get multiple graduate degrees, which led me to very rewarding careers as a school principal and then a business coach. I doubt I'd have achieved as much if not for my principal's recognition of my talents and encouragement to develop them."

Not everyone will see the best in us. What they reflect back may say little about us and more about their perception of themselves. The same may hold true when we ourselves speak harshly or deliver hurtful words to others. In the spirit of the affirming way of life, both in giving and receiving words, the question to always ask is, "Will these words help or harm?" Recognition words always help.

The Power of Recognition Words

Recognition words are purely about recognizing talents, strengths, and positive qualities in others and voicing what we see. Our empowering words can become mirrors in the following ways:

Help Another Know More of Who They Are
My dear friend Lynn was a stay-at-home mom. When her children were well-anchored in school, she decided to go back to college to earn a master's degree in social work. Her

first job was at a social service agency developing programs for at-risk children. She felt both eager and nervous because she'd been away from the workplace for so many years. After she'd been there for a couple of months, her boss, Patty, took her aside and shared a startling observation.

"Lynn, you have a unique smartness. Some people see just the trees; others see just the forest. You have the ability to see both at the same time. You bring a rare sense of problem-solving to developing programs that serve kids."

Lynn was blown away. She knew she had a broad perspective, but had never identified it so specifically. Her boss's recognition of her strength helped her to know more about herself, and made her feel more capable. "Patty's words really stuck with me," she said.

When she moved on to a new job, Lynn recalls the interviewer asking, "What outstanding qualities will you bring to the job?"

Without hesitation she answered, "I'm able to see both the forest and the trees. I have the ability to analyze and problem-solve present-moment issues with long-term consequences in mind." Lynn incorporated the quality her boss identified into her identity. Recognition words not only boosted her self-awareness, they propelled her onto a fulfilling career.

Confirm You're on the Right Path

At one point in my teaching career, I went through a period of questioning: *Am I just teaching subjects, or am I really impacting the lives of my students? Are my efforts actually building my students' confidence? Am I helping them discover their capabilities?* I loved my students, but I felt beaten down by the ever-increasing number of mandates from school district administration.

During that time, I had a special relationship with a third grade student and his mother. In previous years, learning had been a struggle and an unpleasant experience for Ronny. His mother, Claire, was anxious for this year to be a better one for her son. I found Ronny absolutely delightful. He came to school each day with a twinkle in his eye and a song to entertain us. He'd sing, "My name is Ronny Flocks...I live in a box...I hate the smell of socks..." All his classmates would chime in, and it became a happy, daily, laughable moment. I saw not a boy with a reading disability, but a boy who just needed extra support to flourish.

At the end of the year, Claire surprised me with a heartfelt letter of appreciation. She wrote, "With a lump in my throat, I thank you from the bottom of my heart for the way you truly saw and embraced Ronny. You saw the glint in his eye and allowed Ronny to be Ronny. You took an interest in his interests and encouraged both his academic growth and his self-expression. What is exceptional about you is that you make this effort with each and every one of your students."

The message rang out loud and clear after two other parents sent me similar letters. I was fulfilling my mission as a teacher. Their recognition words confirmed that I was doing what I'd set out to do; I was indeed making a difference by nurturing the confidence and unique personhood of my students.

From that point on, I felt more empowered and effective in my career. Those precious letters helped me recognize that my unique talent as a teacher was valued. They confirmed for me that I was on track with my career goal.

Build Confidence

Oprah Winfrey's career as the highest-rated talk show host in American television history was launched by recognition words. I read a wonderful story about how this happened in Marlo Thomas' book *The Right Words at the Right Time*, a collection of personal revelations by over one hundred famous people who were changed by the gift of words. Oprah explains that with much trepidation, she interviewed in 1983 for the talk show, *AM Chicago*. Her competition would be Phil Donahue, the person who created the genre of frank, open conversation for daytime viewing. Donahue was also based in Chicago. At the start of the interview she explained to the station manager, Dennis Swanson, that at her previous job they wanted to change everything about her from her face to her weight and even her name.

Swanson's response surprised Oprah. He told her that she had a talent for connecting with people. He said he didn't want to change anything about her. He just wanted her to share her talent with the show's audiences. "Just go on the air and be yourself."

Oprah says those simple life-changing words gave her the confidence to speak with her own voice. *AM Chicago* became *The Oprah Winfrey Show*, wowing audiences for twenty-five seasons.

Support a Positive Life Change

Tony Robbins, a world-renowned, personal growth seminar leader, often has more than 7,000 in attendance at his *Unleash the Power Within* events. His TED talk ranks as seventh most viewed out of thousands. Tony unleashed his own power thanks to recognition words from a high school teacher.

Growing up with an abusive, alcoholic mother, he saw himself as a clown until his high school debate teacher, Mr. Cobb, recognized his ability to move people with words. In an interview with Carmine Gallo of *Forbes*, "How Raw Communication Changed My Life," Tony quotes the recognition words from his teacher that changed his life: "I have never seen anybody who can stand up and speak with no notes, look around to kids who won't listen, and mesmerize them with just raw communication." Mr. Cobb gave Tony a speech to read called, "The Will to Win," and said, "If the speech moves you, I challenge you to read it in a persuasive oratory competition." It moved Tony to tears and he went on to win first place.

"I realized public speaking was a skill and a gift," Tony said. From that point on Tony refined and nurtured his capabilities creating a rewarding career as one of the most influential personal growth trainers in the world. If not for his teacher's recognition, his life circumstances may have led him down a very different path.

Hearing Again and Again is Believing

When I returned to school one September, I noticed that our principal, Sylvia, had lost weight and was in great shape. "You look fantastic," I said.

"That's because I did my first Triathlon this summer," she beamed.

"Wow. That's amazing. Were you experienced in distance swimming and running?"

"Not at all. I just trained regularly with my friend, and I built up to it."

I was intrigued and inspired. As a non-exerciser, I was looking for direction to become more active. After thinking about it for days, I asked her whether we could compete in a race as a staff.

With Sylvia's support, I found twenty-five other teachers to join us. We would enter a 5K at a nearby college in six weeks. *Could I actually do it?* I wondered. I wasn't a runner. How was I going to run 3.1 miles? I could barely walk that far! Sylvia gave us all training schedules. My teammate Kathy became my training buddy. Four days a week I ran on the treadmill, then once a week we walked and ran outside.

The day of the race, as the runners took off at their different paces, I wondered again, *Will I be able to keep up with Kathy and finish this race?* Yet as challenging as it was, I did manage to finish.

Diane, one of the other teacher-runners, came up to me afterward and said, "I didn't realize you're a runner." Me, a runner? I just soaked her words in.

Kathy and I did two more 5K's that fall. After the second one, when I told my hairdresser Kim about my new running life, she said, "You know my mother did a half-marathon."

Her mom, Carol, was sixty-one, just a little older than me. That night I asked Gus, "Do you think I could do it?"

"Why not?" he responded. "You're a runner."

I approached Kathy and two of our teammates, Jessica and Ryan, and asked if they'd be willing to do a half-marathon with me. They all agreed. Within days we were signed up for Long Branch's New Jersey Half Marathon.

Kathy and I continued our weekly training runs, increasing our distance to six miles, then nine, then twelve. When I told my friend Lynn our latest distance she said, "You go girl! I couldn't imagine doing that at our age. You are quite the runner. When you put something in your mind, you do it!"

Determined and *runner* became part of my identity. Recognition of my capability from friends along the way made all the difference.

Self-Recognition

Seeing how strengthening recognition words can be, we can use them for ourselves. As I pointed out in chapter four on self-supporting words, repeating positive words from others can help us boost ourselves up. We can take a more proactive stance by writing those words down and even repeating them aloud in a private moment.

When Lynn said I was quite the runner and had the determination to accomplish my goals, I repeated her words later when I was alone. *You are a runner, Gail. I'm so proud of you. You will be able to complete the half marathon.* I wrote Lynn's words on an index card and posted it where I'd see it to further feed my confidence.

The next day when I mentioned Lynn's affirmation to my sister, she said, "I think you're just as athletic as my daughters. I could never run like you. I always admire your discipline and determination."

Taking the initiative to repeat those recognition words aloud, write them down, and share them with my sister, supported the knowledge that I had it in me to complete the race. It was tremendous confirmation.

As I write this, it's been five years since completing the half marathon. I know I can run, race, and do much more physically than I'd ever imagined—because I've done it. Hearing the recognition words "You are a runner," over and over helped me cement my new identity and expanded capability.

Ultimately the recognition words you give to yourself will bring you greater self-love and a deeper sense of peace.

 What ability would you like to strengthen? Is there something you've always dreamed of doing? What holds you back? What words of recognition can you offer to yourself? Write them in your affirming notebook.

Tell Them

One summer afternoon, I was doing my three-mile walk around the neighborhood listening to author Ann Patchett on my iPhone. I was about to read her novel *State of Wonder* and was curious about her thinking and research. Ann was being interviewed by Eliza Borne of the website BookPage.com. "What is it about the teacher/student relationship that interests you?" Borne asked.

Patchett passionately spoke of the influence teachers had on her life, including an extra special one. "I was at a writer's conference yesterday in Chattanooga," she said, "and I saw my very favorite writing teacher, Allan Gurganus. We had a lovely half-hour conversation, but I kept thinking, *you have no idea how much I love you. You have no idea how central you are to every piece of how my life turned out.*"

Her answer made me wonder. *Why do people hesitate to express their admiration and appreciation to others? Reserved upbringing? Intimidation? Fear of rejection? Assuming the other person already knows she's great and doesn't need to hear it?* I wished I could have said to Ann Patchett, "Tell him! It means so much."

If I'd had the chance, I would have told Patchett that it's deeply satisfying for a teacher to know his or her efforts have reached their mark. I can only imagine how proud and pleased Gurganus would feel to know that his student, Ann Patchett, a widely respected and revered author, considers his influence key to her success in life.

Tell anyone and everyone who has touched your life exactly what they've meant to you. When you recognize a stand-out strength, describe it to the person. Your words are gifts beyond measure.

The Spill Over

I am imagining the possible trajectory of words of recognition. I'm thinking of Tony Robbins and his teacher's influence. Tony went on to create a billion dollar personal growth empire and in his workshops he's trained over 50 million people from 100 countries. Not only has Tony created an amazing life that he loves, but he's positively affected so many others as a result. And those 50 million people no doubt affected countless others. That brings us to at least 100 million people influenced because one person cared enough to recognize and express the talent he saw in another.

Tony Robbins is no ordinary person, but each of us impacts many, many others. We have the ability to recognize and express the good qualities and talents we see in others so that we can make our own great difference in the world.

Your Takeaways

1. Recognize the stand-out talents and qualities of dear ones and others in your life and tell them.

2. Remember when someone recognizes a strength of yours. Repeat it to yourself and become receptive to their gift.

3. Notice the good things you do, and recognize yourself often in your self-talk.

4. Consider how repeated hearing of recognition words becomes believing.

5. Write the recognition words others say to you and those you tell yourself on note cards. Then post the cards within your sight to visually remind yourself of your strengths and wonderfulness. (I do and those traits eventually become part of my identity!)

CHAPTER 6

Appreciative Words

It was our Jewish holiday of Passover. I'd spent days preparing the Seder dinner for Aunt Lil, Uncle Marty, my three cousins and their kids, and my own family. I set the tables with my best tablecloths and china. I bought fragrant blue hyacinths and budding pink and yellow tulips for cheery centerpieces. I shopped, cleaned, and carefully cooked the turkey until it was golden. We read from our Haggadahs that told the story of our people's exit from Egypt to freedom, and then we ate with relish. After the meal, we laughed and played the game Scattergories for hours. At the end of the evening everyone hugged, and *kvelled* (raved) about the beautiful dinner and wonderful time they'd had, but it was Aunt Lil's call the next day that made the experience complete.

"Gailie, you outdid yourself! No one sets a table as gorgeously as you! The food melted in our mouths. You made us all so happy. What a *balabusta* (great homemaker) you are!"

My aunt's words made me glow. I'd poured my heart into creating a wonderful holiday for everyone and her call showed me how much my efforts were valued.

Appreciative words are words from the heart expressing the value we hold for another's gift—from the simplest of deeds to the most meaningful acts of kindness or compassion. Sadly, it's easy to take kindnesses for granted, neglecting to express genuine gratitude. Heartfelt appreciation, like every other part of the affirming way of life, kindles warmth and can make people feel closer. Pausing to appreciate the kindness of others might actually make us even happier than the receiver. Developing the habit of gratitude is a gift we can give to our self that opens our heart to all there is to appreciate in our life. There are so many opportunities to express heartfelt appreciation.

Words That Say, "You Matter"

Appreciative words give you the chance to reach inside yourself to find words to show people they are valued. It can be for something as simple as holding the door open, offering a sincere smile, or complimenting a new haircut.

Then there are the big moments that can be deeply touching, like when hospice nurses compassionately offered their services to my family during my dad's serious health decline.

Appreciative words are much more than a perfunctory, "Thank you." They acknowledge small and large kindnesses with an extended thank you from the heart. Imagine taking a wholehearted pause to feel and reflect on the kindness and goodness another person may have graced you with. How much more meaningful the interchange is when you extend your gratitude with specific, sincere, heartfelt appreciation.

According to The Random House College Dictionary, appreciation is:

1. an ability to understand the worth, quality, or importance of something or someone.

2. to increase in value.

3. gratitude.

In their *Journal of Personality and Social Psychology* article, "A Little Thanks Goes a Long Way: Explaining Why Gratitude Expressions Motivate Prosocial Behavior," positive psychologists Adam M. Grant and Francesca Gino confirm the impact appreciative words can have. They conducted research on the relationship between helpers and their beneficiaries and found that when helpers were shown appreciation for their services, it motivated them to do more positive work in their communities. Grant and Gino explain that the simple act of being thanked can make helpers feel more valued—and even make some feel they are making a difference in the world.

What happened with my father's health aide, Theresa, is a wonderful example of how appreciation can serve as a motivator. Theresa loyally cared for both my dad and Eleanor for over four years. When their health deteriorated and they went into a nursing facility, Theresa was there daily to feed them, dress them, and tend to their needs. She understood their idiosyncrasies and made them laugh. Because Lois and I and Eleanor's daughter, Lana, lived far away, we were deeply grateful to Theresa. We considered her family and showered her with heartfelt praise.

"Theresa, you are such a comfort to us all. We are so grateful for the way you make sure Dad has his paper every morning and his breakfast piping hot; you know him! And you always have a Diet Coke ready for Eleanor with the TV tuned to Turner Classic Movies. The nurses at the facility tell us what a gem you are and how lucky we are to have you. As if we didn't know!"

Expressing our heartfelt appreciation showed Theresa how deeply her efforts were valued. After my dad passed away and Eleanor moved near Lana, Theresa decided to go to college to earn a degree in social work. I believe our words of appreciation helped her more fully recognize her talents and worth, empowering her to expand her reach into the larger community.

Expressing appreciation says, "I don't take you, your generosity of spirit, your kindness, or your life for granted."

But Many Do

Sadly, many of us take the care and kindnesses we receive for granted. When taken too far, ungratefulness can create bitterness in place of the love we could share.

My running buddy, Kathy, was devoted to her ninety-one-year-old mother. She called her daily, took her to bingo midweek, to church and breakfast on Sundays, and to frequent doctor appointments. After many of their times together, instead of expressing words of appreciation, her mother simply complained, "You never spend enough time with me!"

Kathy often spilled out her heart to me. "No matter what I do, it's never enough. I'm always thinking of my mother and how I can make her happy and more comfortable, but she doesn't get it. She's just a miserable person!"

How different their shared moments could have been if Kathy's mother would have only paused to recognize how fortunate she was to have a daughter she could count on. A few kind words from her lips might have sweetened the bitter pill of their relationship.

Before my dad passed on, my sister and I asked him about his thoughts on life after death. In a choked voice he said, "If there's a heaven, I hope to see my mother again. I was so busy with my own life that I never told her how much I appreciated all she had done for me. I would love to get a chance to tell her." My dad reminded us of the ever-important message to express our loving feelings to those we value while we can.

Expressing Heartfelt Appreciation
Makes Us Closer

How often do we go from experience to experience without taking a moment to relish and appreciate the gifts of the heart others bring to us?

Brian Doyle in his inspiring TEDxYouth@San Diego talk "365 Days of Thank You" (2013), shares how narrowly avoiding a fatal car crash prompted him to think about all the people in his life who meant the most to him. He wondered, *Do they even know how much I value them?* Months later on Thanksgiving, Doyle's thoughts crystallized. *Why limit expressing thankfulness to one day a year?* He decided he would call or sit down with one person a day for a whole year to thank them for the ways they'd touched his life. Following this, he would write them an in-depth acknowledgement of their magnificent qualities and reasons for his gratitude, and then post it on his blog. (Doyle's Blog, "365 Days of Thank You," is a tremendous resource for models of how to recognize and express appreciation.)

Interestingly, Doyle merely stated the number of people he thanked until he got to #170, his dad. "My heart was pounding out of my chest. Voicing my appreciation to my father was even more stressful than coming out and telling him I was gay. I'd never spoken to him this way before." Doyle thanked his dad for everything—the lessons he'd taught him, adventures they'd had, ways he'd shown him to enjoy the beauty of nature, and for his enormous impact upon the person he eventually became.

They embarked on a two-hour conversation about their relationship that ultimately changed the way he and his father related to one another. Doyle says with deep gratitude, "Our bond is more tangible and real now."

Each time we express our feelings of appreciation to others, we deepen the bonds with those who matter most to us. As former Vice-President Joe Biden once said, "What comes from the heart enters the heart."

The Grateful Pause

Brian Doyle demonstrates how feelings of gratitude begin with thinking about the specific things others bring into our lives. Before my dad passed away, I experienced a heightened awareness of the multitude of blessings gratitude brings.

At the time when my dad went into nursing care in his North Carolina retirement village, I lived a plane ride away in New Jersey. Being so far away, I grew very anxious about his well-being. Luckily, in addition to Theresa, his health aide, my father had a loyal and dear friend who looked in on him each day. Carol, the wife of my dad's deceased best friend, called me several times a week to report on his care and condition.

As I drove home from work one late winter afternoon, I composed in my mind a heartfelt thank you to Carol:

Your devotion to Dad means the world to us. I don't know what we would do without you. It's such a comfort to know you are there each day to help him feel connected to who he is beyond his illness. Your calls and reports make me feel like I'm there. When I was

visiting last week, you felt like family to me. There aren't enough
words to thank you! Bless you.

I felt incredibly fortunate that this dear woman cared
so deeply and was there for us, so when I arrived home, I
wrote a note to Carol expressing my heartfelt thanks. Then
it hit me—my thank you may have given more to me than
to her! Expressing appreciation allowed me to take a grateful pause and savor the comfort Carol brought to me and
my family. Though my words were intended to make her
feel loved, being appreciative reminded me of how loved
and blessed *I* was. Expressing my appreciation was a gift for
both of us.

 Has someone touched your life who you'd like to
thank? What would you say if that person were here
right now? If it's possible to relay these words via a
note, a phone call, or in person, why not do so?

The Gratitude Habit

There's a way to turn a grateful pause into an uplifting ritual.
Here's how I do it. Each night as I lay my head on my pillow
I think of at least five things from my day that I am grateful
for—daily achievements and tasks completed; simple things
like a hot shower in the morning and a warm comfy bed;
bigger things like the ability to run and dance and the miraculous healing power of the body; perpetually important
things like the comfort of a sibling, a loving family, the blessing of a child. The list goes on 'til I drift off to sleep.

It has been at least five years since I developed my gratitude habit, and I'm certain it's a major contributor to my happiness. It's helped me scan the world for positives, as author/researcher Shawn Achor recommends in his popular TEDxBloomington talk, "The Happy Secret to Better Work," (2011). Achor says we can actually train our brain to be happy. In his list of five effective things we can do to be happier, number one is to write three new things we're grateful for each day. Doing this for at least twenty-one days, he explains, helps us develop a more optimistic, happy mindset.

Reflecting on what's good in our lives and giving thanks for those things makes us happier and gets us into the habit of noticing the good others bring into our lives.

The Goodness Others Bring to You

Each day of our lives includes countless interactions with others that can make life lighter, easier, and happier—if we notice. I'm talking about everything from ordinary moments that may barely register to special experiences that bring deep pleasure each time they're relived in our mind.

- What are the ordinary moments in your life that you're truly grateful for?

- How do you express your gratitude toward others?

There are plenty of chances to say how much we care, if we stay open to them. Keep the above questions in mind as you consider the following opportunities to express appreciation:

Shared Experiences

Gus and I have friends who often invite us to their vacation home in Vermont. We so enjoy our time there that I email them as soon as we get home. I try to be as specific as possible when I thank them.

"Thank you for giving us the most wonderful time. It was a joy to buy all those fresh vegetables at the farmer's market. Gus and I both agree that *Singing in the Rain* was the best musical we've seen in ages. He says he will gladly babysit the dogs if you ever need someone. He's in love with them. How lucky we are to have such easy-to-be-with, generous friends as you!"

Even when I'm the one inviting people, I like to reach out with appreciative words to acknowledge the pleasure of being together. "It was so much fun kayaking with you," I texted my friend Jerè.

"I always enjoy nature outings with you," she warmly responded.

A downside of being appreciative is it can set us up for disappointment if we expect others to do the same. For many years I misinterpreted the lack of a follow-up thank you from others as not being valued. Conditioned by Aunt Lil, I was hurt if someone didn't contact me the next day to show they appreciated my efforts. It left me feeling cold.

My friend Jill described such a situation. She had made an eightieth birthday party for her older brother and his family. Knowing how elegant she is, when she said she put a lot into preparing the party, I knew it was an understatement. At the end of the evening Jill says, "My brother's daughters and wife thanked me profusely, but I never heard from them afterwards. Each day my husband, Tom, would ask, 'Have they called you yet?'"

"'Oh, they'll be sending an email any day now,' I'd respond. But they didn't. It was eating away at Tom. Day after day he'd inquire and each day he'd become more agitated."

"They should have extended themselves because you extended yourself," Tom chided. "No more putting yourself out for them."

A seemingly little thing like a call, text, or note the next day, can actually be a big thing to the giver, and in turn, to your relationship with them. Tom's point of view is one many of us might take—that others should do as we do. But the reality is others do as they do, and so they may not always meet our expectations.

I've learned after many experiences of disappointed expectations as a giver to remind myself that not everyone realizes how much an extended thank you means.

A Service Provided

How often does someone provide a service that we take for granted? After all, we're paying money for their assistance.

I was in a Bed Bath & Beyond looking for a clothing steamer. When I couldn't find what I was looking for on the shelf, I asked a young man working there for help. He told me his name was Tyler and proceeded to spend thirty minutes looking online, showing me options, and helping me decide which model might best meet my needs. As it turned out, the one I decided on wasn't available through their store so he encouraged me to order it elsewhere. I was very touched by his service.

"Thank you, Tyler, for giving me such patient attention. Someone else might just have given up, but you cared that I got what I was looking for. The store is lucky to have such a fine employee as you."

"You have no idea how much that means to me," he said. "Nobody has ever acknowledged what I do here. In fact, just the other day I got contemptuous stares from a grandmother and mother when I was creating a bridal registry. They were like, you're a boy, what do you know!"

"Well, I can see you're going to be successful at whatever you do because you connect well with people, and you put in the effort that's needed to get a job done."

"You made my day!" Tyler said.

My affirmer-self couldn't stop thinking about how much my words meant to that young man, what little effort it took to give them, and the good feelings we each enjoyed as a result.

Kindness/Kind Words

Kindnesses are so much a part of the everyday fabric of our lives that they can be invisible to our hearts and minds. They don't have to be.

Entering a building, someone holds the door for us. A smile and words such as, "Thank you. That's so kind of you," enable us both to turn an ordinary moment into a happy one.

A former student sends an email saying that thinking about what she learned during our time together motivates her to work harder in middle school. I write back to let her know how much her words mean. Both our days shine a little brighter.

When my cousin Debbie was recently hospitalized for multiple myeloma—cancer of the bone marrow, an unexpected kindness gave her a boost that she valued as much as her medical treatment. While undergoing chemo and a stem cell transplant, Debbie remained in a satellite of Sloan Kettering Hospital for three weeks. Only her immediate family could visit. We were all deeply worried about her and wanted to give her hope. Our nephews Russell and Brian decided to create a video for Debbie so everyone in the family could send their love and healing wishes. Over thirty of us contributed. Russell and Brian spiced up the video with a humorous battle skit where Debbie's healthy cells won out. My cousin was overcome with tears of joy when the video arrived.

Within minutes of receiving it, Debbie texted them, "I am touched beyond words by your video! Thank you for creating something so beautiful for me. I am overwhelmed by all the love. You have no idea how much strength and hope this gives me!"

My cousin crystallizes the value of appreciating kindness. "Each time I think about the kindnesses everyone's showing me, I feel the love. When I let them know how much I appreciate what they've done, I feel closer to them and I feel stronger."

Our Relationships

Hailey Bartholomew, in her TEDxQUT talk, "365 Grateful Project" (2014), tells a touching story of how a daily search for things to be grateful for helped her see her husband in a new light. She found it disappointing that her husband was unromantic. One evening during her yearlong project, she noticed as her husband was serving dinner, he gave her the biggest piece of pie. Another day, when she complained that their air conditioning wasn't working, he arrived home with two pints of ice cream. Tearfully she revealed that her expectations of him as a romantic had stopped her from appreciating the sweet ways he actually did show his love. She says, "I wouldn't have seen it if I hadn't been looking."

Before my gratitude practice became a habit, like Bartholomew, I often focused on what I expected from my loved ones, missing all the good stuff right in front of my nose. We often forget that it is the key people in our lives who sustain us. What would our lives be without the love and loyalty of family and friends?

Like Bartholomew's husband, my husband tends to be unromantic, but he is extremely considerate. Now I realize how lucky I am for that and I tell him so. Instead of letting judgments cloud my mind, I look for the good and keep my focus on that. I can watch just so much TV, but Gus could watch all night. If I say I'm ready for bed, he turns the TV off with no complaints and finishes watching his programs downstairs. Now I'm able to recognize how much he's willing to respect my needs, so I say, "Thank you, honey. I know you'd rather keep watching. It's so considerate of you to go downstairs."

"You need to get your sleep," he says sincerely. His response shows me that my appreciative words soften his sacrifice.

My sister calls me every day on her way home from work. She listens wholeheartedly when I'm upset, and we discuss every part of our lives. Although we are different from each other, we realize the preciousness of our relationship. As our mother's daughter, affirming is as much a part of who she is as it's a part of me. After Lois' long day of giving to others as a nurse counselor, she still finds time to listen, and my appreciative words reenergize her.

"Loey, I don't know what I'd do without you! Even though you were tired, you gave me all the time I needed to talk through my stuff."

"Why wouldn't I, Bubby? You do the same for me," she says. Our affirming words to each other keep our heart connection strong.

Rather than focus on the small, annoying things my son occasionally does, I think about how he makes time to call me most days. I tell him how grateful I am for those calls. "You are such a loving son," I say, and the warmth I feel back from him shows me that my words feed our closeness.

We may think people already know how we feel about them, but that's not necessarily true. Why not speak up? After all, who doesn't like hearing good stuff about themselves? Expressed appreciation exponentially multiplies the love and tenderness we share with those who mean the most to us.

Positive Influence

At the 2017 Golden Globe Awards, Viola Davis presented Meryl Streep with a Cecil B. DeMille Lifetime Achievement Award. Davis began with a confession of her admiration for Streep. "When you and I were working on the set of the movie *Doubt,* each night my husband asked me, 'Did you tell her how much she means to you yet?' But I didn't."

On this night, however, Davis's husband threatened to do it himself if she didn't. As she gave Meryl Streep the award, with a voice filled with emotion, Viola Davis said, "You make me proud to be an artist. You make me feel that what I have in me, my body, my face, my age, is enough. You encapsulate the great Emile Zola quote, that as an artist, 'I came to live out loud.'" Before that moment, Meryl Streep probably had no idea she'd been such an influence on Davis's sense of self as an actress. How valued she must have felt to learn her acting provided so much more than entertainment.

Theo had four inspiring professors who influenced him in college. Whenever he'd call home, stories about them enlivened his conversations. As the time drew near for him to graduate, we felt indebted to these professors for their life-shaping impact on our son's development and direction. Gus and I decided to invite them to lunch the day before graduation to express our gratitude. To our surprise and delight they all accepted.

When the professors arrived, we hugged, exchanged some funny stories about Theo, and sat down to enjoy drinks at a cozy corner table. After we connected and relaxed together for a while, I pushed my chair back, rose, and said,

"My husband and I are overwhelmed with gratitude for your positive influence on Theo's life. You all made him passionate about reading, analyzing, and writing clearly.

"Bob, it was your conversation with Theo on the second day of school that inspired him to switch from a communications major to English.

"Thank you, Tim, for insisting he take your class to improve his grammar, did he ever need your help!

"Kim, your feedback and opportunities to make his papers better fed his determination and his sense of capability as a writer.

"Len, the many hours you spent philosophizing about life with Theo meant so much.

"Most importantly, you all valued his leadership skills while accepting his quirks, like propping his feet up on the desk. You have been the best part of Theo's education and will forever be dear to our hearts."

The professors appeared as touched as we felt appreciative. They told us we were the only parents ever to extend such a thank you. From the conversation that followed we could see that our words and gestures of gratitude were as wonderful a conclusion to their connection to Theo as it was for us.

Who do you want to reach out to so you can express appreciation for a shared experience, a service provided, a kindness/kind words, your relationship, or for being a positive influence? Jot their name and reasons for your gratitude in your notebook, then call, text, email, write a letter, or express your appreciation in person.

You Give a Bag of Clothes, You Get a Bag of Clothes

As my sister was raising her three daughters, she discovered a truism that became a watchword for both of us. When the girls outgrew their clothing, Lois loaded the clothes into large plastic bags and passed them on to friends with younger daughters. Inevitably, within days, another friend with girls a little older, brought Lois bags of beautiful clothes, enough to replace the ones her girls had outgrown. It seemed kind of miraculous.

From then on, when Lois or I did something kind for someone else and received an unexpected kindness in return, Lois said, "You give a bag of clothes, you get a bag of clothes."

As you become conscious of the goodness others bring into your life, from the smallest to the most major gestures, relish how fortunate you are. Express gratitude from your heart, and the blessing of the bag of clothes will be yours.

Your Takeaways

1. Create a daily gratitude practice where you mentally go through your day and give thanks for all the small and large blessings you experience.

2. Take a grateful pause to notice and savor the goodness others bring into your life, then tell them!

3. Express an extended thank you for shared experiences, services, kindnesses, your relationships, and positive influences.

4. **Remember, whatever you give out, you get back in joy.**

CHAPTER 7

Encouraging Words

I'm what you'd call a late bloomer. I remained in a ten-year relationship until I was in my mid-thirties, knowing in my heart of hearts it wasn't right for either of us. James filled an emotional void and anchored me. Yet I watched from the sidelines as friends my age got married, had children, and bought homes of their own, while I stood still, living with James, feeling like a failure.

One afternoon, driving home from work, I noticed a new condo development with units for sale. Just for the heck of it, I took a tour. Fireworks flashed in my mind. I could see myself living there—alone. But how could I reveal my true feelings to James? He would feel so betrayed. And how would I manage on my own?

Bursting to talk to someone, I dropped by my friend Jan's house. She and her husband, Gary, were our best friends, and I knew she would help me decide what to do. As she painted a bench on the porch of her sky blue Victorian home, my feelings spilled out.

"I found a place I want to buy!"

"Wow, that's great!" Jan put down her paintbrush and motioned for me to sit with her on the porch steps.

"Without James," I said more quietly.

"Whoa. What's going on?"

"You know how confused I've been about my feelings for James...but the truth that I couldn't even admit to myself is I can't see myself ever marrying him."

Jan listened attentively as I unloaded my doubts, fears, hopes, and dreams.

"I will be really sad to lose you and James as a couple because we have so much fun together," she said. "But maybe it's time. The condo sounds perfect! You can do this. When you make the move, I believe your life will begin to shift in the direction of your dreams."

Jan's encouraging words gave me permission to break free from my holding pattern. Though I'd received encouragement from many others during my limbo years, Jan's words were pivotal because they matched my readiness to go for my dreams.

Encouraging words are possibly the most precious affirming words of all. They are like rainbows in the clouds when we're coping with life's challenges or dreaming of new possibilities. Encouraging words build hope, courage, perseverance, and confidence when we need inspiration the most. In essence, encouraging words say, "You can do this." Our words can help people move through their stumbling blocks. Becoming a great encourager starts with being a good listener. Four effective ways to encourage are: focus on strengths, help create a new narrative, offer reminders of past successes, and hold a broad vision for what's possible. Best of all, you can use these techniques to encourage yourself.

Be a Rainbow in Someone's Clouds

Of all the forms of affirming, encouraging words may be the most life-changing. In moments of fear, doubt, and indecision, when we are feeling most vulnerable, encouragement from others can be a life-saver.

Maya Angelou's famous speech "Be a Rainbow in Someone Else's Cloud" is a powerful nudge to encourage generously. Angelou says, "I have had a lot of clouds in my life, but I have had so many rainbows. When I have to get up on a stage to speak, go to direct a movie, to teach my classes, I bring along everyone who has ever been kind to me. I say, 'Come with me, I need you now.'" The encouragement Maya Angelou received sustained her, and so she encourages all of us, "Prepare yourself so you can be a rainbow in someone else's cloud."

Her beautiful metaphor reminds us that we all have cloudy periods of despair. Words of encouragement can part those clouds during our darkest days and reveal a rainbow of possibility.

In his TEDx talk, "Words of Encouragement Can Last a Lifetime" (2015), Colonel Glennie Burks, tells an impactful story of his rainbow-in-the-clouds person. When he was in sixth grade his parents divorced, creating many struggles for him. Sitting out in the hall while his parents met with his teacher during conference time, he overheard his teacher say, "Don't worry about your son; he's talented, and he's going to be OK." Burks says this simple statement filled him with confidence that propelled him forward throughout his life. He often returns to those words during challenging times. As a military leader during the war in Iraq, he described how a superior told him, in front of his entire staff, that his plan to move five thousand displaced civilians stunk, and that he didn't know what he was doing.

"I went to my office and thought, I can't let this situation define me. I reminded myself of my teacher's words from forty years before to get me through." He proudly shared a letter of praise from his superior on the eventual success of his plan.

Colonel Burks' final words to his audience were, "Be an encourager, especially to young people at risk. Seemingly simple words at critical moments can be huge life uplifters." I love his story because it shows how long-lasting and life-impacting encouraging words can be.

Support for Facing Challenges and Realizing Dreams

Y. Joel Wong, positive psychologist at Indiana University, speaks of the five invaluable strengths we support in others when we encourage: *confidence, hope, perseverance, courage, and inspiration.*

These inner qualities enable us to handle two major life circumstances where we need support the most:

- Facing and working through challenges, big and small

- Achieving goals and realizing dreams

Our greatest struggles can help us become our strongest, best selves. It's when we struggle or strive that encouraging words make the most difference.

Facing Challenges

None of us are untouched by challenges, whether they're relationship problems, job or money issues, an accident, or ill health—we all face life challenges. And it is during these times, when we need our inner resources the most, that they may be least available. Supportive, sincere words from others may be just what we need to bolster our hope and reconnect us to our inner strength.

In her memoir, *Guided Cure,* Paula Beiger writes about how encouraging words gave her the hope and courage she needed to persevere through her battle with colon cancer. She raves about the technicians who treated her with radiation for six long weeks. "They made one of the scariest times in my life bearable." On her graduation day from

treatments, Paula received a card with heartfelt words from
two caring professionals who'd come to know and admire
her fighting spirit.

One wrote, "We know you'll make it through this. You
make the best of whatever is thrown at you. You are strong
and beautiful, a confident go-getter, and we know you will
always turn those lemons into lemonade. Remember you
have two earth angels on your side."

The other said, "You are an extraordinary woman who
will find the positive in any situation. I have no doubt that
your attitude, drive, and determination will cure you! We've
both grown by knowing you!"

Although Paula felt frightened and weak, her technicians recognized the strengths that made her successful in
her fight. She writes, "If I'm ever having a bad day, I read
their card and gain all the confidence I need to carry on."
This is the magic of encouraging words.

Even when dealing with minor challenges, encouraging words can be just what we need to raise our spirits to
help us manage things better. Shortly before an evaluation
conference with our principal, my teammate Janet was a
mess. "Sylvia left before the end of my lesson. She didn't
get to see the kids apply the skill I taught. She's going to
think I'm a terrible language arts teacher and my evaluation is going to be horrible."

I thought differently. On several occasions Sylvia mentioned to me what a great job Janet was doing with her
bilingual students. I knew our principal had eyes that saw
the best in her. I also was aware of how thoroughly and in-
sightfully Janet prepared her lessons. "Don't worry. Just the

other day, Sylvia spoke to me about how impressed she is with the way you reach your students and with the progress they're making. All your other evaluations have been so positive. I'm sure this one will be, too."

"You think so, Gailie? I really needed to hear that."

Encouraging words helped her go into her conference more confidently and with a much-needed positive perspective. As hoped for, the conference went very well.

Achieving Goals and Realizing Dreams

Striving to make our dreams a reality is where the passion and fire of our lives ignites. Each step we take empowers us to take another. But what about when we don't know where to begin? When we don't think we're capable of making our dreams happen? When we're not seeing results? I know what it's like because I've always been a dreamer, and some of my dreams were like juicy, ripe apples on high branches in the sun. I lacked the confidence I needed to climb my dream tree and pick those luscious fruits.

One of my dearest and most difficult dreams I yearned to accomplish was writing this book. For years, I collected ideas and jotted them down. The problem was, I'd never studied writing and my self-doubt kept me from making progress.

The climb to fulfillment began with encouraging words from my son. "Mom, there's an article on the front page of the paper about Carol Kivler and the books she's written. Call her. I know she'll help you get started writing your book."

Carol, a leader in the mental health field, is my hair stylist's mother. As Theo predicted, when I called she generously agreed to be my writing coach.

Each month I was thrilled just to come up with ideas to weave together into a chapter, but Carol clearly wasn't as impressed. "Your chapters are really long. You're too wordy. Your sentence structure needs work." Her feedback showed me how and where I needed to grow, but I felt discouraged. My ideas didn't wow her; my writing came up short. So I turned to the people who love me and who have faith in me and my dreams.

"Keep working at it, and you'll get better," said my husband. "You weren't a talented teacher overnight. It takes time. I know you can do this."

"Your message is important. Look at the positive influence you've had on Theo and all your students with your affirming approach. Keep writing! People need your message," said my sister.

I joined a writer's group. They were harsh with their criticism of my writing, at least initially. "You sound preachy," said one member. "I can't believe you really experienced that," said another. Yes, I needed their honest feedback to improve, but I also needed to hear what I was doing right to strengthen my belief in myself. Luckily, there was plenty of that as well.

"Excellent fact-based research to back up your ideas. Flows nicely from section to section. Keep it up," said Rod, our writing group leader.

"Love the content in the chapter on dealing with criticism," said MaryAnn, another group member. "It's dead on. Delivers major insights in few words. It's a whole new way of thinking for many people."

Their encouragement meant so much to me that I wrote their words in bright-colored markers on index cards and hung them on either side of my writer's desk.

Fulfilling a dream takes persistent, consistent hard work and encouragement. I was strengthened to do the work because of encouraging words from my trusted circle of readers and dear ones.

Who in your life needs encouragement now to get through a challenge or help in persevering to achieve a dream? What words do you think they need to hear? You might want to jot them in your affirming notebook.

Do you need some encouragement yourself? Who are some trusted people you can turn to for encouraging words?

You Can Do This

Facing challenges or working to make a dream a reality can sometimes feel like we're driving a car with a flat tire, on a deserted road, in the pitch black night. But the faith of someone who knows us well and says, "You can do this," can be just what we need to inflate that tire, get moving, and add some light to the road ahead.

The poem, "Mother to Son", by Langston Hughes, replays in my mind when I want to summon inner resources. In it, a mother who has had a life of struggle lectures her son to keep going and never give up, no matter how challenging life gets:

Well, son, I'll tell you:

Life for me ain't been no crystal stair

It's had tacks in it

And splinters

And boards torn up...

But all the time

I'se been-a-climbin' on...

And sometimes goin' in the dark

Where there ain't been no light...

So boy, don't you turn back

Don't you set down on the steps

'Cause you finds it's kinder hard

For I'se still goin' honey...

And life for me ain't been no crystal stair.

I imagine this mother with a life of poverty and hard breaks, and I soak in her message—if I can make it in the worst of circumstances, you can too. No matter how hard the challenge, how distant the dream, don't give up. Keep on moving.

The letters of encouragement Paula Beiger received from her radiation technicians reinforced her inner strength to take whatever action was needed in her battle with colon cancer. You're holding this book right now, thanks to my loyal family and friends whose cheers led me to keep moving through my many moments of doubt. This is the exquisite power of encouragement.

Where it Begins

Like Maya Angelou, we feel a heart full of gratitude toward those people who are rainbows in our clouds, but how do we find encouraging words to be a rainbow for someone else? The desire to be a supporter of others is your most powerful asset. The skill of encouraging begins with a compassionate heart and a willingness to listen generously.

Generous Listening

Dr. Rachel Naomi Remen has been a model to me of deep compassionate listening. As a cancer patient counselor, medical professor at the University of California San Francisco (UCSF) School of Medicine, and a lifelong sufferer with Crohn's Disease, she teaches medical students and faculty the greatest gift they can give their patients—the art of listening generously.

She became known as the doctor who listened because she recognized there was more to healing a sick person than curing the body. Through her own suffering from Crohn's Disease and her experience undergoing multiple surgeries, she understood that people confronted with a life-threatening illness need a compassionate listening ear to mobilize their full strength and the strength of their families. They need support to wade through their fears, anger, and hurt, so that they can in time access their inner wisdom and peace.

Who of us hasn't suffered illness, seen a loved one suffer, or gone through a loss that shakes our very foundation? It is from our own humanity that we, like Dr. Rachel Naomi Remen, can offer our compassionate listening ear.

Listening to an inspiring interview on the NPR radio show, *On Being*, I had the opportunity to learn from Dr. Remen how she trains medical students to be generous listeners. She begins with a simple instruction. "Remember a time when you experienced a disappointment or loss of a relationship, a life-dream, or even a family member. Who helped you at that time? What did that person say and do that made a difference?"

Next she has the students reflect on a difficult time when someone wanted to be of help but wasn't. She asks, "What did that person say and do? What message did he deliver? How was the message delivered?"

Her students then meet in small groups to talk about their losses, with one direction—listen generously. Out of this experience the students generate a list of the things that either helped them in their loss or missed the mark. Here are some of their realizations:

Things the person did that helped:

- Listened to me as long as I needed to talk

- Talked to me in the same way after my loss as they did before my loss

- Gave me their full attention

- Sat with me

- Touched me

Things the person did that didn't help:

- Gave me advice without knowing the full story

- Made me feel the loss was my fault

- Talked about themselves more than listened

- Seemed distracted

I connect to what Dr. Remen says and teaches because in my own struggles, the generous listening of others has made all the difference. I most appreciate when I can see on the other person's face and hear in their words their deep concern for me. It means so much when they listen for as long as I need, and when they show their faith in me to find my own answers to make it through my challenge. It also helps when the person rephrases what I say so I can objectively hear my own thoughts. After feeling fully listened to, I can better receive any insights or hope the other person offers. Is it any wonder that we feel a deep heart and soul connection with people who listen to us this way?

The generous listening I've been gifted with during moments of need have been literal life-preservers. My mission is to offer this kind of deep, compassionate listening to those who turn to me for support, especially my family and friends. Our own encouraging words can bloom from our experience of feeling fully heard.

When Theo was a junior in college, compassionate listening played a critical role in helping him through a crisis. One night he called home distraught. "I just can't take it. I'm all shaky. I have to come home for a couple of days."

He'd just broken up with a girlfriend and was shouldering many leadership responsibilities plus a heavy, coursework load. To make matters worse, he was in a state of sleep deprivation, living with a roommate who played video games until all hours of the night. The alarm and stress in his voice told me I needed to take a couple of days off from work and give him my full attention. And that's what I did.

Sitting next to him on our living room couch for hours at a time, or walking with him in our local park, I listened as his thoughts and feelings tumbled out. Looking back, I can see that my deep caring and undivided attention allowed him to release his anxiety. He needed to express his worries, fears, and catastrophic thinking. I didn't interrupt, which helped him open up even more.

"Mom, I don't feel like myself. I don't know how I can go back to my situation. Mitch is f—— inconsiderate. I'm afraid my grade point average is going to drop."

Theo had lost touch with his usual confidence and inner anchor. I could see he needed help viewing his situation from a larger perspective. Even though I was shaken by his anxious state, I knew it was up to me to help him remember his resilience.

"Theo, you're doing the healthiest thing you can right now—getting your feelings out and coming home to catch up on your rest. You're rebuilding your inner strength. You're taking action to care for yourself. I am confident you will feel better and find a solution, just as you have in the past. This is *temporary*. It will pass, just like steam on a bathroom mirror."

Theo was relieved to recognize that nothing stays the same, and to remember that he'd made it through other times of crisis. Once his anxiety shifted, he came up with a solution that worked for him.

Seeing this crisis through the lens of "It's temporary," became wisdom he could turn to and pass on to others.

What are some ways you can hone your listening skills so you can become a more compassionate listener? You may want to jot your ideas down in your notebook.

How can what you've been through help you be supportive and encouraging to someone going through a crisis?

What challenge or crisis have you experienced that you can now look back on as temporary?

Credible Encouragement

To reach the person who needs your support, your words must be believable. Y. Joel Wong's research shows that if the believability gap is too great between your encouragement and the person's view of themselves, your words will just sound like, "Blah, blah, blah."

A former student, came to visit me at school one afternoon. Tommy expressed his anxiety about getting into a college of his choice and needed reassurance. He'd always been a hard worker and would be a good fit for college. If I said, "Don't worry. You'll get into any college you apply to," my encouragement would have fallen on deaf ears, because Tommy knew learning didn't come as easily for him as for others. Yet, he had lots of initiative and would often come in at recess time for extra help days before a test. He had a strong desire to do his best. It was from these memories I spoke.

"I don't think I've ever had a student willing to give up as much recess time as you to do well on tests, and you got the results. I remember you as a highly motivated hard worker. Colleges look for students who are willing to work, not just the ones who get the grades without effort. I'm sure there are many colleges who will want a student like you."

"Yeah, in high school I was on the honor roll all senior year. I hope some colleges see what you see in me."

Reminding Tommy of truths about himself gave him faith in his own ability. The words he heard were believable because they were true. By the time he left, he was smiling and cracking jokes.

Four Ways to Rouse the Sleeping Army

When we encourage others through their challenges or toward their dreams, we help them mobilize their inner resources to feel whole and strong in the face of doubt. We help them connect to the essential qualities of *hope, confidence, perseverance, courage, and inspiration.* Our support activates these traits like a sleeping army awakened by the bugle to battle. Listen for what people need from you. Sometimes they might just need to hear their own words as they share their concerns. At other times your words will be the ones to give them strength. You'll intuitively learn what to give as you practice generous listening.

The following ways to encourage have made a big difference in my life, and I now use them to support others. Because they are so effective, these techniques are also used in counseling. The motto for each approach encapsulates its powerful message.

Strengths Focus: "You have what it takes."

Years ago I worked with a bright, effective teacher who helped struggling writers excel. Kim herself was struggling, though. In her late thirties and longing for a child, she'd just experienced the failure of her third in vitro attempt to conceive. When I saw her disappointment, I tenderly opened a conversation to see how I could help.

"We've been trying for so long," she said. "Maybe we're just not meant to have a baby."

It wasn't like Kim to give up. She was one of the most determined people I knew. I sensed that emphasizing that quality might be what she needed.

"That's so hard, Kim. You know, what I admire so much about you is your resilient, persistent spirit. You bounced back from a messy divorce. You then found your just right sweetheart of a husband. You managed to get a Master's in Educational Administration and Supervision even with the stress of trying to conceive. And I couldn't get over how you transformed Catalina, a below-level writer, into the winner of this year's essay competition. You seem to always find a way to reach your goal."

"Aww, thanks, Gail. You have no idea how much I needed to hear that. Maybe I need to give this some more thought."

The next morning I stuck my head in Kim's room and saw her intensively researching alternative ways to get pregnant. She was a fighter, and the encouragement she received helped her tap into her reservoir of strength. Eventually she found an egg donor and gave birth to a healthy, beautiful baby boy.

Kim's resurgence of hope and determination were fueled by all the people in her cheering squad. I was delighted that I could be one of them to remind Kim "she had what it took" to overcome her challenge and make her dream a reality. Even the slightest supportive words may be just what someone needs to find her inner strength.

New Narrative: "This is who you are."

Financial difficulties can be an issue for many of us at one time or another. While Gus and I have had financial concerns before, it was when we started planning my retirement that I went into a downward spin. Sitting down to go over our income and assets, we realized how much the investment property that was supposed to support our retirement had plummeted in value. I saw my dreams shatter like a thousand shards of glass. After thirty-eight years of working, there suddenly seemed no chance we'd own the lake house we'd hoped for or the bucket-list vacations we'd pictured. I felt nervous and teary. But my family saw the larger picture. They were confident we'd be fine and tried to reassure me.

"With your pension alone you have more money than many people I know who are retired and living comfortably," said Lois.

"You don't have to worry," Gus told me. "We have the resources. We're going to have more than we do now because you won't be paying into the pension or your health benefits."

"Mom," Theo said, "When I interned in the governor's office, constituents would call in with no health insurance or pension. You're fine."

No matter what they said, I couldn't believe the positive spins they were casting.

It was my friend Ryan who helped me to gradually come out of my darkness. "I can see how scary it feels to you," he said. "But I know you're a resourceful person. If you need to, you can earn money when you're retired. You are a spiritual seeker who knows miracles are available to us when our mind focuses on positive possibilities. You may be surprised by all the new opportunities that will be available to you when you look at your situation with fresh eyes. Just keep bringing your most positive sense of self to every moment."

His words became the glimmer of that rainbow peeking through my clouds. Ryan reminded me I was a person capable of creating the reality I chose. His words literally lifted me out of my fears and returned me to a larger perspective on my life. I hung up a note card in my bedroom closet, "Keep bringing your most positive sense of self to every moment." I reread it numerous times a day until it indeed became my reality. Ryan's encouragement helped me remember who I was regardless of my circumstances. When I did retire, we were fine financially. I adjusted my thinking to let go of the lake house dream and realized I could still make vacations happen. That is the power a new narrative can create for us. It reminds us of "who we are" and of our infinite possibilities.

Past Successes: "You've done it before."

As we walked around the high school track, my friend Kathy vented. "I am so unhappy with the way I look. I don't know where that thin girl I used to be went. I am at least twenty pounds heavier than the day I was married!"

"I understand how you feel. What helped me was joining Weight Watchers."

"Yeah, but you didn't have as much weight to lose."

I sensed she was discouraged and needed to access her inner faith in herself. "You have been my inspiration when it comes to walking. Your daily habit made me want to develop the habit too. I couldn't get over how you went from walking one mile, to three and now you even run three miles. You did it with exercise. Why can't you do it with dieting?"

"Huh. I didn't think of it that way. Maybe I could go with you to Weight Watchers to get me going."

Kathy was ripe to take action. She did so well on Weight Watchers that she joined their staff. Reminding her, "You've done it before," helped empower her to believe she had the persistence and discipline to take control of her weight.

Envisioning: "I can see you doing this."

My brother-in-law and I have never seen eye to eye. In fact we rarely talk to each other. The exception was a memorable conversation we once had supporting each other's visions. George, a talented designer, and a passionate basketball coach to his three daughters and countless teams, had a dream of opening his own gym. He worked at a job where he felt unappreciated. He believed his gym would enable him to contribute to his community doing what he loved to do most. For more than a year, he devoted every spare minute to researching and creating a highly professional business proposal. He just needed an investor who believed in his project as much as he did.

One evening while we sat together on the screened in porch of his lake house, I had the opportunity to look through his proposal. I could see the vision he laid out clearly on each of his painstakingly created pages. "George, your plan is so impressive. I am confident you're going to find an investor."

"Yeah, do you know anyone?" he said, chuckling.

"I don't. But "I can see" that big beautiful green and white building you designed filled with happy kids running up and down your shiny basketball courts. You're going to get an investor, you'll see."

"I hope so," George said. I could see in his face that the vision I'd conjured had connected.

"What's your dream?" he asked, surprising me. He'd never taken an interest in my life before.

When I described my vision for this book, he said, "You're going to write and publish it, you'll see." It was the most personal and meaningful conversation we'd had in his thirty years of marriage to my sister.

George did eventually get the investor he needed and now is the proud owner of Courtside, a successful recreation center serving his community. I have no doubt that he benefited from all the people who believed in his vision. I was proud to be one of them.

When we listen to what's really important to someone and encourage him to describe his dream in detail, we help him to "see himself doing it." Our faith kindles his faith that what he dares to dream is possible.

Who would benefit from your generous listening or a reminder of who they are using one of the mottos? Jot some ideas in your notebook to think about what you'd say, then do it.

What motto would you like to use to encourage yourself?

Difficult Encouragement

Not all people who need our encouragement will open up to us with their struggles. When people we care about are in deep pain, encouragement grounded purely on generous listening and loving care is what they need most.

My friend Janine described how she learned this lesson, which I in turn learned from her. Janine's friend and neighbor Lola was a vibrant contributor to her community, until a freak accident claimed the life of her nineteen-year-old son. Drapes drawn, not taking phone calls, not even taking the food left on her porch, Lola retreated into a dark place.

Janine was deeply concerned about her friend's heartbreaking depression. She decided to bang on her door till Lola answered. With dark circles under her eyes, hair a mess, looking like she hadn't showered in days, Lola finally came to the door. Janine hugged her tenderly and said, "Can I come inside? I brought you some soup." Lola let her in. They sat together in her darkened living room. Janine compassionately asked, "How are you doing?"

"Not good. You can see I'm barely alive."

"Well, I know you're a strong person, and you *will* get through this."

"I'm not strong. This has depleted me to my core. Did you say that for me or for yourself? I just need someone who really understands."

Initially stung by Lola's words, Janine recognized her friend needed her compassionate empathy and company, not words to lift her out of her feelings. "Lola needed to be with her pain in order to move through it," Janine said. "My words may have made her feel she was handling it wrong. After that, I'd visit her, kiss her cheeks, and tell her how sorry I was for her suffering. I saw that genuine care, just being there with her, was what she needed. Over time Lola got better. Compassionately listening guided me intuitively to give her what she needed most."

Our perspective on our role in the healing process when someone we care about is suffering is crucial. Dr. Rachel Naomi Remen, in a *Shambhala Sun* article "Helping, Fixing, or Serving?" explains three different ways we see ourselves in relationship with others. Helping and fixing are based on coming from a place of our strength and the other's weakness. In serving, the wholeness in us serves the wholeness in the other. We are compassionate because, we too, have our own pain, limitations, and darkness. Dr. Remen says fixing and helping create separation between people. Serving creates profound connection.

I developed a fixer mentality from a young age because I so wanted to fix my mother's bipolar suffering. From her dark, stale-smelling bedroom, she'd call out to me, "Gailie, help me, please; I'm so depressed." I'd try everything I could think of to lift her spirits and release her from the black hole that seemed to be swallowing her up. I'd write her hopeful notes, reassure her, or help her get up and take a shower. I saw my mother as broken and wanted to fix her so that I could have a mommy and she could be happy. She reached out to me for help, and I offered the only kind of encouragement I could imagine as a young person.

I still have remnants of that fixer mentality. But I have learned to empathize rather than fix when I recognize emotional pain in another's face, voice, or words. I remind myself that the more I just listen and care, the better I can serve the wholeness in the other person.

Keep the following in mind when you want to serve someone you care about who is deeply suffering:

- First, ask what they need. It may not be conversation or a meal. It may just be hand holding or to be alone.

- Be there for them. People who are in deep pain want to know someone's there for them who understands the depths of their suffering. The words we use when we mean to be encouraging may, in fact, merely be a way to avoid our own uneasiness.

- Allow them their suffering. People need time to heal. A woman who just lost her son isn't ready to hear she's strong. She needs time to mourn.

- Be patient. Quick solutions are more for the discomfort we are feeling ourselves. Our caring presence and willingness to listen deeply to their words and body language can guide us to give what they need most.

I have come to realize, the deeper the suffering of another, the fewer words needed.

Self-Encouragement

Every word of support and kindness you extend to others you also extend to yourself. We take our own words in subliminally, feeding our subconscious mind with the positive thinking we're offering. Encouraging others teaches us how to encourage ourselves.

A friend tells you the upsetting news she received at the doctor's office. You listen compassionately because you totally understand how scary it is to discover you have a health problem. If it hasn't happened to you personally, you've seen someone dear to you suffer. Being empathic with her suffering is opening you to being empathic with your own suffering.

I used to assume the worst and become a bundle of nerves with the slightest negative report from a doctor. Then when I learned it was nothing, I'd judge myself mercilessly, "You overreacted again!" Now though, after living the affirming way of life for so long, I compassionately accept my feelings and comfort myself as I would another. "I understand how you feel, Gailie. You have good reason. But it's going to be OK," and I feel more relaxed.

I find when I'm scared or upset, I say to myself something like, *Debbie had scary health news and she got through it*. Or, *You calmed yourself enough to talk through the issue you had with Judy without putting her on the defensive. You'll be able to handle this issue as well.* I realize I'm encouraging myself with past successes, my own or another's I've observed.

Every time we join with someone's vision and truly see it and feel it, we are also supporting ourselves in believing that our own heart-held dreams can come true. I knew my brother-in-law was going to open the gym he imagined. I felt a bolt of inspiration during our shared encouragement, that if I worked hard like he did, my dream to write this book was possible too. Whatever we give out, we give to ourselves as well.

If we don't feel hopeful and positive, how can we offer hope and positivity to anyone else? Whether we take in the support we give to others as a new way of talking to ourselves, or choose to intentionally bolster our own spirits when needed, it's empowering to realize we have within us the just right words to encourage ourselves and the people we care about.

Your Takeaways...

1. **Recognize others' suffering and difficulty pursuing dreams as opportunities to give encouragement.**

2. Become a generous listener. Others want and need your empathy and understanding more than your advice.

3. Communicate the message, "You can do this."

4. Notice and name another's strengths in handling a challenge so she can know, "I have what it takes."

5. Help others remember "who they are" regardless of their circumstances.

6. Show another his past successes so that he might realize, "I've done it before, so I can do it now."

7. Hold a new vision of possibility for someone who feels stuck by weaving a scenario that matches his dream so he can feel, "I can see myself doing this."

8. Offer your compassionate understanding presence to those you care about when they are in deep pain.

9. Imagine that every time you encourage someone else you are also encouraging yourself. Say to yourself the encouraging words you need to hear so you will have faith in yourself and your future.

CHAPTER 8

Healing Words

I had three mothers, and from each of them, a lifetime of resentment to release.

My real mother, Selma, as loving, kind, and accepting as she was—was usually unavailable. She was either depressed and helpless in bed, or manic and shaming me with the outspoken things she'd say in our community. I blamed her for not teaching me the life skills other mothers seemed to teach their daughters. I felt like I absorbed her depression and helplessness, and my life was handicapped because of it. Creating the life I yearned for was a long hard struggle, and in my mind, it was all her fault.

Aunt Lil, my substitute mother, always knew just the right words to say to comfort me when I was worried; the problem was the way she treated my mother. When my family arrived at her house for Thanksgiving, and my mother looked inevitably disheveled, Aunt Lil would shriek, "Selma, you can't come in my house like that! You look like a bag lady."

My mother, easily hurt, would turn to me and ask, "Do I really look that bad?" Shame crept over us both like a dark cloud. I felt her shame as if it was my own.

"You're not so beautiful yourself with those fat legs," my mother would retort to Aunt Lil, and back and forth the sparks would fly. For me the day was ruined, and inside I fumed.

When I was older and working as a teacher, my mother would call me sounding *femisht,* (all shook up). "Your aunt makes me feel like a nothing. She tells me, it's no wonder I lost your father to that woman. She says, 'What man would want a woman like you?'"

My mother's frequent upsetting calls turned me into her protector. Why didn't Aunt Lil realize my mother couldn't help being the way she was? Resentment made a nest in my heart. Long after my aunt passed away, the hurt and anger lingered.

Eleanor, my third mother, came into my life when she married my father. She was a cultured New Yorker, generously taking us to Broadway shows and restaurants. As a twenty-one-year-old, I was awestruck experiencing Tavern on the Green, The Russian Tea Room, and The Rainbow

Room. From the start, though, we seemed to be vying for my dad's attention. I always felt close to my dad growing up. He was my healthy role model. When he left our family for Eleanor, I agonized over maintaining my bond with him. Because of Eleanor's own emotional baggage, she became affronted by my attempts to have personal conversations with my dad. Nuclear meltdowns often followed. "I guess I'm not wanted here because you'd rather be with your *daddy*. Nobody cares about me and how *I* feel," she'd bellow, storming out of the room. A version of this scenario went on every time we were together throughout all the years of their marriage.

Not to ruffle his wife, my dad avoided any real contact with me. I was angry at Eleanor for not allowing me to have a relationship with my dad. I resented the way her emotional neediness darkened the times we spent together. It took me days to recover after seeing them. Her careless upsetting words lingered with me like scars from chickenpox.

Throughout a major part of my adult life, I relived my hurts, anger, and frustration with all three mothers. These feelings impaired me from living freely, much like the broken ankle that once kept me from dancing and doing what I loved to do most.

To live the affirming way of life and express our unique selves, we need to get out from underneath negative feelings and resentments that block our inner peace and loving hearts. Forgiveness is the

way to release our hurts and gain freedom. It is a lifelong choice and practice that can bring us the peace and love we desire. Forgiving our parents for their imperfections and for the hurts they may have caused us is fundamental. To forgive our parents is to be, in a sense, reborn. Self-forgiveness is at the root of forgiving others for the least to the worst of injuries. As we become kinder to ourselves and are more able to own the hurts we've caused others, we become more able to forgive those who've hurt us too. Forgiveness opens our hearts to a well of positive feelings from which our affirming words can flow.

Healing Ourselves Opens the Way

The affirmations and kind words we freely give to others come from a well inside our hearts. When our well is even partially filled with good and loving feelings, we can dip inside for some reviving words to lift a spirit, offer encouragement, or deepen connections. But being human, we've all experienced hurt, pain, and for some, even abuse. I know what it is to endure mental and emotional pain that becomes convoluted into shame, guilt, and self-blame. Others, whose stories I've listened to, have suffered sexual and physical abuse, and even sadistic cruelty. Hurt and abuse drain our heart-well dry, so loving ourselves or anyone else becomes not only a challenge, but almost impossible.

A life-changing book that started me on my long road to healing is *You Can Heal Your Life* by Louise Hay. In the last chapter she tells about how being diagnosed with cancer opened her to dig deeper into her life. She had been raped at age five and endured sexual and physical abuse throughout her childhood. Years later, as a teacher of mental and emotional transformation, she realized she had to clear the blame and resentment she rightfully felt towards her parents and those who'd harmed her. Louise Hay says, "I was literally eating my body with cancerous growth because I had not forgiven." It's not that she was to blame for her illness. Not at all. But she believed the stress of past and present traumas impacted her body.

I am a student of *A Course in Miracles,* a self-study spiritual thought system that teaches the way to universal love and healing through forgiveness. From the lessons I've learned that we are on earth to love ourselves, to love those who are both easy and hard to love, and to live lovingly. Forgiveness is the way to dissolve our hurts and refill our well. It helps us free our minds and emotions from lingering negativity, so we can feel the love, and have access to the affirming words we seek. Forgiveness is a choice, an ongoing life decision that brings us peace and gets our hearts flowing again.

Getting to Forgiveness

Any emotional and mental suffering I struggled with seems minor after listening to TEDx forgiveness talks from people who endured physical and emotional harm. I have come to understand my own healing process better through the commonalities I observed in listening to their healing processes.

Colleen Haggerty, in her TEDxBellingham talk, "Forgiving the Unforgivable" (2013), told the story of how she

lost her leg in a car accident at age seventeen. One snowy
night, as she was driving on a highway with her older sister, their car spun out of control. Haggerty stepped out of
the car to flag down help, when a driver named Harvey
hit her, severing the lower half of her left leg. For the next
fifteen years, anger, resentment, and rage toward Harvey
consumed her. It impaired her relationships, and her fear
of drivers on the road frequently overwhelmed her to tears.
She finally realized she needed help.

In her therapist's office, she had a chance to let down
the emotional defenses she had built up over all those
years. Expressing her pain in a safe place with a trusted
guide brought her to the realization that releasing her
bitterness was a gift to herself. She made a decision to do
whatever work it would take to forgive, not for Harvey's
sake, but for her own.

On the fifteenth anniversary of her accident, Haggerty
called Harvey and left a message. She felt she needed to
let him know the devastating effect he'd had on her life
so that she could forgive him. She assumed he had gone
on with his merry old life and didn't give a damn about
what happened to her. When Harvey called back, Haggerty
screamed, "Do you know who I am? Do you know what
yesterday was?" His sobbing response opened her heart to
meet with him.

She had plotted revenge, but when they finally met,
Haggerty saw a thirty-six-year-old who suffered from ulcers,
a failed marriage, depression, and regret about that fateful
night. Her rage flew out the window. "I met two new people

that day," she says, "Harvey and my compassionate self. In order to hold anger, resentment, and sometimes hate in my heart, I had dehumanized him. When I looked at the situation through the lens of connection and opened my heart to his story, I opened myself to Harvey's humanity." As the waters of forgiveness began to flow, it was as though she came to life again. Within a year, Haggerty met the man who became her husband, started a family, and found her life's work.

A similar shift occurred for Sammy Rangel, a man who'd been severely sexually and physically abused. In his TEDxDanubia talk, "The Power of Forgiveness" (2015), he explains how he was raped repeatedly by an uncle and inhumanly treated by his mother until he was eleven. At that point he couldn't take it anymore. He ran away from home, and found survival in a gang. Rangel repeated the violence he knew all too well. By his late twenties he was so brutal that no prison wanted him. He was forced into a treatment program, which changed his life.

Rangel's counselor asked him to talk about his mother. Through unexpected tears he described repeated beatings on the head with a belt buckle, pulled patches of hair, not being allowed to eat, being forced to wet himself, no bathing, wearing unfit clothes to school, and the shunning by peers that followed.

Rangel was taken through a powerful process where he imagined asking his mother why she treated him so badly. The turning point came when his counselor asked, "Have you ever hurt anyone the way your mother hurt you?"

Tearing up, a flood of realizations came to him. He'd abandoned his own children. He had brutally beaten people as a gang member and prison inmate. He had been both victim and victimizer. Experiencing the common humanity he shared with his mother and all his victims jolted him out of the box of pain he had called home. Through an ongoing process, Rangel took a new path. He says, "Since then my life has been one long apology."

Teaching others about the path of forgiveness has become the life work of both Haggerty and Rangel. Haggerty's book, *A Leg to Stand On: An Amputee's Walk into Motherhood*, and Rangel's, *Fourbears: Myths of Forgiveness*, help them spread their healing messages.

The turning point for each of them reminds me of the process through which we find compassion and affirming words for others. When we're willing to look more broadly at the people in our lives, we are able to see more of who they are, and it is from this expanded view that we gather the positive thoughts from which to affirm.

When Haggerty and Rangel were ready to see the common humanity they shared with the perpetrators of their abuse, their frozen hearts split open and began to melt. They continue to spread healing words of forgiveness because of the love and happiness forgiveness helped them find.

A Framework for Forgiving

I found it enlightening to look at the process by which we get to forgiveness. The Enright Process Model of Forgiveness, developed by Robert Enright of the University of Wisconsin-Madison, illustrates this beautifully. He created his model based on his work with incest victims, children in areas of violence, emotionally abused women, and people in drug rehabilitation.

Enright emphasizes the importance of understanding what forgiveness is not. Forgiveness does not mean forgetting the harm the offender caused, condoning their actions, or reconciling with them. It does not require the offender to apologize or take responsibility for what happened. They may not be capable of doing so, nor may they be trustworthy, and some may no longer be alive. We forgive as a gift to ourselves.

The Enright model has four phases that clarify the process both Colleen Haggerty and Sammy Rangel went through and that any of us go through in getting to forgiveness.

PHASE 1: The Uncovering Phase
(Identifying and Feeling Your Pain)

Uncovering begins when we allow ourselves to talk about the suffering or harm another person caused us. This often happens when carrying the pain becomes unbearable, or when we find ourselves obsessed with thoughts of the person we believe robbed us of living happily and freely.

When her out-of-control fear of cars could no longer be ignored, Haggerty went for therapy to talk about the anger, sadness, and bitterness she'd stuffed away for years. When Louise Hay's body caved in to cancer, she chose to face the abuse she suffered at the hands of her parents.

Identifying the cause of our suffering can start with journaling or in conversations with trusted family or friends, but the most effective uncovering is facilitated by ongoing work with a good therapist.

We start by recognizing that suppressing pain is the tip of the iceberg. The deeper uncovering happens when we become brave enough to feel and express the hate, anger, shame, blame, and resentment locked inside. It might mean crying, screaming, pounding, or pacing for however long it takes to release and understand our buried emotions. Haggerty says that feeling her emotions was scary, but it opened the way for her healing.

There is no set amount of time to work through feelings. It can take months or years. The one thing we can count on, is that going through the process fully can give us the gift of a happier heart.

PHASE 2: The Decision Phase
(Choosing to Forgive For Yourself)

Fred Luskin, co-founder of the Stanford Forgiveness Project, says our deepest suffering comes from the hurt feelings and thoughts that get triggered each time we relive the past. In the *Greater Good Magazine* article, "Fred Luskin Explains How to Forgive," Luskin helps us understand that *our own feelings* are the source of our pain, which is our most important reason to choose the path of forgiveness. Our offender may not deserve forgiveness, but we deserve to be happy. Haggerty says, "I didn't forgive Harvey for his sake, but for mine." Forgiving was about focusing on her deepest relationship with herself. Because releasing pain is a gradual process, forgiving is a choice we make over and over again.

PHASE 3: The Work Phase
(Seeing Your Offender in a New Light)

When we've uncovered the fullness of our feelings and chosen to forgive for our own inner peace, we are ready to focus on our offender. Continuing to blame them squeezes our hearts shut. The way to open our hearts is to find compassionate understanding for the person who did us harm. Unimaginable? Here's how the process worked for Haggerty and Rangel.

When Haggerty met with Harvey, she learned how much he had suffered since the night of the accident. She saw not an ogre, but a human being who truly regretted his fateful actions. She felt surprising compassion for his years of anguish. This compassion pried open her heart. Most of us don't actually confront our offender as Haggerty did, but it's still possible to find compassion.

Rangel did just that. When his therapist had him imagine his mother's response to the question, "How could you do that to me?" he saw for the first time that she was a flawed human being just like himself. He realized that his mother had probably been abused, too. The clincher for him was when he was asked, "Have you ever hurt anyone the way your mother hurt you?" With that, Rangel's point of view expanded. He saw the common humanity that he and his mother shared. He felt great sadness at committing similar crimes.

Seeing our offender from a broader perspective helps forgiveness flow. As we shift our view of the person who harmed us, we shift our view of ourselves. Haggerty and Rangel both talk about creating a new story about painful experiences. They each say loud and clear to let go of the victim story, and refuse to allow yourself and your life to be defined by past awful times. Because of their choice to do the continual hard work of forgiveness, they each define themselves as heroes. In the same way, we can each be the hero of our own story.

PHASE 4: The Deepening Phase (A New Life Purpose)

Once Haggerty and Rangel experienced the healing balm of forgiveness, the mission for each of them became helping others to do the same. Their books, inspirational talks, and organizations help others understand this transformational process. They show how freeing up the energy expended by holding onto anger, resentment, and hurt can be channeled into positive new ways of living for one's self and the benefit of others.

Resentment and hurt never go away completely. All of our life experiences become part of the fiber of our brains, bodies, and emotions. When old thoughts and painful feelings are triggered, we can recognize that they're normal. We can then choose to release them in a way that brings us peace. In essence, we are rewiring our brains. I have found the following actions helpful:

- *Mindfulness practice:* when disturbing thoughts arise, refocus attention in the present moment. (STOP! DON'T GO THERE! can refocus you.)

- *Yoga breathing:* slow deep inhaling and exhaling can help relax body, mind, and emotions.

- *Journaling:* writing our feelings and thoughts on the page helps us release old thoughts and emotions and gain perspective.

- *Walking in nature:* can be soothing and anchors us in the world rather than in our thoughts.

- *Dancing:* responding with our body to the rhythms and lyrics of music takes us out of our thoughts and can elevate our emotions.

- *Talking to a trusted person:* similar to journaling, we can express and release the thoughts and emotions that are being triggered, and gain perspective through the caring listening and wisdom of someone we trust.

There are many books and websites available to help you release stressors. You might also find that working with a good therapist can make a difference. Just know that forgiving small offenses again and again is a way of life that opens up the love in your heart.

What, if any, anger or hurt toward someone do you need to unburden to regain your peace of mind and heart?

How might you uncover your feelings?

Who can you turn to for help with the process of forgiving?

Forgiving Our Imperfect Parents

I hate to admit this, but it took me well into my fifties to forgive my mother and Aunt Lil. I blamed my mother for needing me to live with her when I graduated college after my dad left, and for my late start marrying and having a family. I blamed Aunt Lil for pressuring me into taking care of my mom when I was struggling to establish my own life. I blamed my mother for being a model of helplessness whenever I felt incapable of creating the life I really wanted to live. And I blamed Aunt Lil for saying cruel things to my mom that I internalized as if they had been said to me.

My mom died at sixty, six months before I married Gus. Aunt Lil died five years later, at sixty-one. My resentments lingered long after they were gone because I continued to be swept up in emotional drama and pain primarily around the difficulties in my relationship with my dad and Eleanor. Though I acted as a loving and competent mother, teacher, and wife, inside I was a mess.

On and off throughout my adulthood I sought help from therapists, and often the conversation veered to one of my four parents. I talked, recounted, cried, judged, and stepped back for perspective. It took years for me to work through my resentments, but when I found the right therapist and stuck with therapy, I eventually found peace, a flowing happy heart, and forgiveness for each parent.

Part of the peace I made with my mom and Aunt Lil after their deaths came from talking about the good they'd brought into my life. When I realized my mother also was my role model for affirming others, it was as if a life sentence had been commuted. She had done something good! Her affirming words became my greatest asset in relationships. Aunt Lil was truly a mother substitute. She taught me things my mother couldn't—like entertaining beautifully, as well as the blessing of family devotion. One of my greatest joys is creating large family meals for my cousins and their families.

Joy and forgiveness came to my relationship with my father when Eleanor became less mobile. They lived in North Carolina, a ten-hour train ride from my home in New Jersey. When travel became hard for Eleanor, she agreed to let my dad visit us on his own. He was eighty-one and far less consumed with his work as a chemical industry consultant. He started taking more interest in my sister, me, and his grandchildren. I found such relief talking with him about all those years he was distant.

"I can see that was hard on you," he said, "but I always loved you and your sister. Eleanor had a difficult mother. It made her emotionally needy. She means well."

Though I wanted an actual apology from my dad for all the years I felt I had suffered, I got something better. But it didn't happen right away.

When my father visited, before he'd go to sleep, I'd hug him and say, "Love you, Dad."

He'd accept the hug and say, "Right."

Right? What kind of goodnight was that? But I hung in there, and after a while he came around, and I finally heard the words, "Love you too, Dear."

Those words were gold to me. I repeated them over and over in my mind, because I'd yearned to feel my dad's love for so many years. For me, hearing was believing.

Each time he visited he became more expressive. A couple of months before he passed away, lying in his bed in the nursing care unit, he said the words that made my heart complete. "I am so proud of my grandchildren, not because they're successful, but because they're good people. And I'm most proud of you and Lois for the wonderful mothers and people you are."

My dad's affirmations helped me forgive him. Because I could finally feel his love, I was at peace in our relationship.

After my dad passed on, I made peace with Eleanor. At that point she had Parkinson's and lived in a nursing care home. Her emotions were tamed with medications. As I continued to do my daily readings of A *Course in Miracles*, the focus on forgiveness as a path to love and peace helped me realize my lingering anger and upset toward Eleanor needed clearing for my own peace of mind as well as hers. I made a decision to forgive and bless her daily. Using the Lovingkindness meditation practice as abridged by author Dani Shapiro, between slow, deep breaths I'd say, "Eleanor *is safe*. Eleanor *is happy*. Eleanor *is strong*. Eleanor *lives with ease*." I visualized her smiling and imagined hugging her. Over time the words I repeated became my true feelings, and when I visited her, I hugged her and felt an easy warmth flow between us.

My choice to forgive, combined with my daily practice, turned my resentment into traces of sediment in a calm stream. The good will my meditation practice brought out toward Eleanor helped me think about the good things about her: She always wanted to be close to me; she introduced me to cultural experiences that brought me joy; she was generous with gifts of clothing; she took good care of my dad.

When I felt competent and empowered to shape my life, I was able to let go of my victim mentality, which kept me feeling at the affect of my four parents' imperfections. I forgave each parent when I could. Forgiveness has no timetable. In spite of the difficulties they each created in my life, I learned to feel their love, and that is what I return to now when each of them comes to mind.

Self-Forgiving

Where does forgiveness begin? When we're able to feel compassionate understanding for those who've wronged us? Is it when we've learned to forgive ourselves for being imperfect? There's actually no one beginning place. There can be many. The one thing for sure though, is when our heart opens with compassion for another or for ourselves, the stone begins to crack.

I suffered deep guilt for the way I hurt and devalued two people who were important in my life. The first was James, my long-term boyfriend. I mislead him with false hopes for at least eight of the ten years we were together. I tried to tell him from time to time that I didn't see us marrying and that I wasn't in love with him the way he was with me, but he didn't take me seriously. Near the end of our relationship my guilt turned me into a wisp of my real self. When I finally gathered the courage to act on the truth and break up with him, remorse was my constant companion.

My self-recrimination tape played endlessly: *You didn't appreciate James' love. He was so pure-spirited compared to you. You wasted his life and your own. You may never find another person to love you the way he did.* My inner critical voice felt like a jellyfish sting to my heart.

The second person I hurt was my mother. Nine months before Gus and I were to marry, my mother developed congestive heart failure. After she was released from the hospital, she was too weak to take care of herself and came to live with me. She couldn't have been sweeter or more appreciative. Any meal I made for her she *kvelled,* (showed complete delight) saying it was delicious and perfect. Anything I did for her, she thanked me profusely. Yet I felt burdened. Planning my wedding was supposed to be the happiest time in my life, but my mother's neediness made it difficult, like so many other times before. She stayed with me for two months, spent a couple of weeks with my sister, and then went on to Aunt Lil's.

Shortly after arriving at Aunt Lil's, my mother called and said, "Gailie, I'm ready to come back to you. I've been away a month, and I'm most comfortable with you."

"Ma, you can't come back yet. I'm going away with Gus for a long weekend. Come on. Can't you let me have a little pleasure for once in my life? I always have to take care of you. I want to spend time with Gus."

Two days later at Aunt Lil's, my mother died in her sleep from a massive heart attack.

For a full year I suffered clawing guilt for my unwilling-ness to be there for her. *You're all about you!* I'd scream in my head. *Now Mommy is gone and you can't tell her how much you love her. Nobody is as uncaring a daughter as you!* I cried frequent tears of shame for being so self-centered.

My behavior with my mother and James was crushing because it went against my core values. I strove to be loving, kind, and caring in my relationships, and for the most part that's who I was, but not with them. My lifelong resentment of my mother was stronger than my care for her. Protecting the security I had with James was more important to me than being real and honest with him.

"True self-forgiveness is often a long and arduous pro-cess. It involves inner self-examination and can be very painful," says Julie Hall and Frank Fincham of the Univer-sity of Buffalo, in their self-forgiveness research.

And painful it was. My inner voice was agonizing to live with so I unloaded my feelings with my sister and close friends who saw the goodness in me that was dimmed in my own sight. They could see I had understandable rea-sons for my choices, and though they helped me have some compassion for myself, I needed to accept responsibility for the suffering I'd caused my mother and James. But where to start?

I began working with a good therapist to better under-stand my motives and needs. I also needed help embracing my goodness and my strengths. It's hard to forgive yourself if you feel like an unworthy, horrible human being.

I made a decision to not repeat with others the behaviors I regretted. Being there for the people who were central in my life was important to me. I also recognized that being more honest and having greater integrity were essential for my self-respect.

After I left James, when I discovered the need for my own self-supporting words to replace the strengthening compliments he had given me, I consciously practiced speaking to myself in the loving tone he so often used. I did my best to focus on what I did right or well. I spoke to myself encouragingly as I would've to one of my students or friends. *I'm proud of you, Gail, you did what you said you would do today.*

Enright's Phases of Forgiveness make sense of the steps I took to make peace with myself.

- First came the painful *uncovering*, as I cried and lamented my insensitivity. Talking to close ones and a therapist over extended time helped me release my feelings and understand the ways I judged myself and why.

- My *decision* to forgive myself emerged when I realized all the pain my thoughts were creating for me and that I deserved a break for being imperfectly human.

- My *work* was to focus on uncovering more of my goodness, so I had reason to support and affirm myself.

- The *deepening* involved understanding my core values and my behaviors that went against them. I was now ready to make a commitment to not repeat behaviors that contradicted my values.

Being alive means that every day you get small moments to practice giving yourself a break for being human. You're ten minutes late picking your son up from school; you forgot to buy the toothpaste for your spouse; you said something thoughtless to your friend; you burnt dinner; you backed into a car in the parking lot; and on and on it goes. Self-forgiveness is not about excusing your wrongs; it's about accepting the fullness of your being, your strong points and your weak points, and again and again committing to learning from your humanness and working at doing better. Part of doing better is taking responsibility when you do something wrong and sincerely apologizing.

The beautiful thing about self-forgiveness is the kinder and more understanding we are with ourselves, the more loving compassion we have to offer others through our actions and our words. That's what the affirming way of life is all about.

Is there something lingering in your heart and mind you need to forgive yourself for? What self-compassionate words can you offer yourself?

Do you need to offer forgiveness to someone inwardly or actually? What might you say or do? You may want to journal on these.

Helping Those We Care About to Heal

The bonus of working hard to find compassion for our imperfect selves and those who've wronged us is that we now have a tender heart to offer others. Compassion means to suffer with, which is exactly what another person needs most when they are in emotional pain.

I remember getting the call that my dad had passed away. I was at school and went off to an empty office to cry in private as I listened to the details. When I returned to my classroom, my students had been taken to the lunchroom, and my friend Jessica was in my classroom with open arms to envelop me. "I'm so sorry," she said, with pure kindness and empathy. "I know how much you loved your dad. Don't worry about your students. We'll take care of everything." She showed such care, I knew I wasn't alone.

When you're in the position of giving the way Jessica was, your heart goes out to the other person so fully that it's expressed in the tilt of your eyes and mouth. It's in your voice, "Oh, I'm *so* sorry," or "Oh, *no*," said soothingly like you would to a child in distress. It's in your body as you give a hug, put a hand on the other person's arm, or move closer. And it's in the words offered from your empathic heart, "What can I do for you?" It's being there to check on them, and not forgetting their pain lasts well beyond the moment you discover it.

As Dr. Rachel Naomi Remen says in her comforting book, *Kitchen Table Wisdom*, "Perhaps the most important thing we ever give each other is our attention. And especially if it's given from the heart." To just listen and truly care about what another person is going through, is one of the most healing gifts a person can offer.

Openness to our own and others' suffering is an important step in moving beyond resentments and regrets.

It enables us to refill our well with positive thoughts from which our affirming words can flow.

Your Takeaways

1. Look inwardly and ask yourself, "Am I carrying hurt or resentment that is limiting my inner peace and joy?" If so, find a good therapist, trusted person, or a journal to begin the process of uncovering your pain.

2. Remember that forgiving others is foremost a gift to yourself.

3. Work at forgiving your parents, if need be, to free up your good energy to connect more lovingly with them and others.

4. Work on forgiving yourself.

5. Take responsibility for your wrongs to others and apologize when you can. Remind yourself that being human means making mistakes. Choose to learn from your humanness.

6. Offer whole-hearted listening to help others heal.

7. Be patient. Healing is a long, yet essential process.

8. Be open to share the positive feelings and positive words that will come from your freed up heart.

CHAPTER 9

Words for Our Children

No one is impacted by our words more deeply than our children. Their sense of self is grounded on the words we use to describe them. If we call them kind and helpful, that is how they will know themselves. If we use names like mean and selfish, that too will become their identity. For that reason, our children need affirming words more than anyone else in our lives.

Two of my fifth-grade students come to mind when I think of the impact of parental words. Maddie's and Michael's parent-teacher conferences were back-to-back. I began, as I did in all conferences, with an anecdote describing one of their positive qualities in action. Two positive stories. Two very different responses.

"Maddie amazes me," I said. "In our reading group, she is raising the bar for the others. Her insightful reading responses are pushing the others to think more deeply and put more effort into their responses."

"Thank you, Mrs. Siggelakis," her mother said, beaming. "Maddie always gives 100 percent to whatever she does. My husband and I are very proud of her." *Maddie is so lucky to have a mother who recognized her best qualities,* I thought.

Next was Michael's conference. "Michael is a talented debater," I began. "I can count on him to get the class talking about ideas. We were discussing the qualities of explorers when he questioned if explorers who stole native people's land were worthy of learning about. He led the class in a great debate."

"That's good, but he's just plain lazy!" his mom said. "I wish he'd put as much time into studying for tests as he does into talking. I tell him all the time he'll never get a good job someday because he's too lazy." Sadly, I could hear his mom's voice in the words Michael used to describe himself. "I'm stupid. I never do well on tests." How could Michael consider positive possibilities for himself when his mother didn't?

Bring every practice of the affirming way of life to your children. The shift starts when you view your children with kind, loving

eyes, focusing on what's positive in them rather than what's not. Name their strengths so your children can recognize their own capabilities. Listen when they speak to show them their thoughts and feelings matter. Listen without judgment to create trust. Express appreciation so they feel valued for who they are and what they contribute. Motivate them by noticing their hard work so they develop persistence and believe they have what it takes to succeed. Model positive self-talk so they can learn to affirm themselves. Bless them by envisioning their best life every day.

Parental Perspective

Being a positive influence on our children's sense of self and sense of possibility is one of the most important gifts we offer them. Helping them know they have the right stuff to handle the myriad challenges of life is to give them super-sized powers. But this may not come naturally or easily. With all the demands in our lives—work, money, health, relationships, emotional issues—who has time to think about how our words shape our children's lives?

Add to this our parental baggage from our own childhoods. Many of us were guided by criticism. When I searched the internet for coping with critical parental voices, Google found twenty-nine million results! If we don't pause to consider how we impact our children, we may unconsciously repeat our parents' critical style, even though this is not our intention.

In our desire to help our kids develop and become their best selves, we often focus on what they still need to do to be better rather than what they're already doing well. What message does that communicate? For some kids the message is, "You're not good enough now." One mother in my parenting workshop said, "I can't help myself. I see where my kids are not doing well in school and I want them to do better. I know they'll feel more confident if they improve, so I say things like, 'Don't you listen to your teacher? Are you paying attention? You've got to try harder.' I guess I'm more focused on what's wrong with them than what's right."

This mom hit the nail on the head. We want so much for our kids to do well in life that we often focus on how they can improve rather than recognizing the wonderful qualities that make them who they are. Our kids need us to see the good qualities they already possess because if *we're* not seeing them, *they're* not seeing them.

We fortify our children when we notice their goodness, their abilities, their uniqueness. When we help them recognize their positive qualities and strengths, we prepare them with the provisions for tackling the multitude of challenges they'll face on their life's journey. We do this by shifting our focus from what's wrong with them to what's right.

Eyes for Strengths

When my son was in first grade he had difficulty focusing, he couldn't sit still, and he called out often in class—all to his teacher's displeasure. As a teacher myself, it was very disturbing to constantly hear negatives about my child. I wondered, *What am I doing wrong? Why can't she see anything good in Theo?* When he started coming home from school and telling his father and me he was a bad boy because of all his timeouts, I realized I had to do something.

Besides looking further into his inability to focus and its effect on his school life, I made Theo's sense of self my top priority. I talked to Gus and close family and friends to gain perspective on who our boy was beyond his school challenges. Someone suggested reflecting on Theo's positives in a notebook to counterbalance the negative feedback from school. My list looked something like this:

- He's honest. He tells us when he gets in trouble.

- He has a cheerful disposition that makes us happy to be with him.

- He bounces back quickly from disappointment.

- He has a strong memory for information that interests him.

- He's loving and appreciative.

- He expresses himself well.

It was a relief to recognize that my boy was so much more than the challenges he manifested in school.

Our kids have many great traits for us to focus on. It's just a matter of pausing to notice. Grab a notebook like I did and write down your child's positive qualities. Ask yourself:

- What are my child's social, emotional, intellectual, physical, and moral strengths?

- What talents does she have?

- What do I adore about this child?

- What do I admire in his character?

- How does this child touch my heart?

- What challenging qualities now may become strengths in adulthood?

- What positive things do others have to say about my child? Ask others who know your child well.

Here's a list of some qualities to get you started:

Social-emotional: friendly, kind, compassionate, helpful, generous, fair, good sportsmanship, encouraging, good listener, good humor;

Intellectual-personality: curious, creative, responsible, reliable, adaptable, hard-working, bold, independent, gentle, determined, disciplined, optimistic, happy;

Physical: athletic, graceful, coordinated, a talent for dancing or other physical activities;

Talents and Skills: art, math, science, computers, music, creative writing, mechanical abilities.

Maggie McMahon, has developed a wonderful way to emphasize her kids' strengths. In her article "Strengths Based Parenting: How to Build on the Positives," she says she uses the Gallup Strengthsfinder books to help identify strengths in everyone in her family. McMahon then hangs each person's list on the fridge as a source of positive reinforcement and a declaration of who they are.

As we set our sights on our kids' strengths we begin to perceive our children differently. We see them with a deeper appreciation for their uniqueness. This shift in perspective becomes a source of joy, pleasure, and pride for us. But our real purpose is to help our kids better know their own strengths.

Nurturing Strengths Confidence

Your basic tools to help your kids see their shining qualities are the Four S's for crafting words of affirmation introduced in chapter 2:

- *Start simply* by choosing one or two qualities or *skills* in your child.

- Be *specific* so that he too will see his strength in action.

- Be *sincere* in the quality you affirm. Kids can see right through phony words. Let your tone of voice sing your pride.

Here is a way I used the Four S's to nurture Theo's confidence when he labeled himself as bad. From the list I generated of his positive traits, I chose "expresses himself well" as the upside of the behavior he was getting in trouble for. His articulate speech became something that Gus and I could easily highlight and praise. At dinner when Theo shared information he'd learned at school, I said, "You explained things so clearly it felt like I was there learning with you." He sat taller in his chair. Continuing to give him simple words of sincere affirmation helped him see himself in a new light.

The following week, his teacher called, and to my surprise, raved about the way Theo entertained the class during his hobby presentation. When he got home I said,

"Mrs. R. said you got up and spoke like an expert about baseball. She said you were really funny and made the class laugh. That's you. You have a talent for speaking well."

"I know," he responded devilishly. His pleasure was obvious.

That night I called my dad, who valued being articulate as a sterling strength that would get a person far in life. I described Theo's teacher's compliments in Theo's earshot, so he'd hear my pride and hopefully feel proud.

It soon became a habit for all of us in the family to affirm Theo's ability to speak well. Today it's one of his greatest assets.

Jessica Abbott, a contributor to Disney's parenting website, babble.com, explains a great way to make focusing on your children's strengths a habit. In her article, "The Rubber Band Method Changed the Way I Parent," she offers a simple way to remember to compliment your child: Wear three rubber bands on your wrist that you move to the other wrist each time you recognize one of your child's strengths.

Abbott said she used to criticize her kids when they didn't do what they were supposed to do and took it for granted when they did. The rubber band approach reminded her to affirm them for what they did right, rather than just criticizing them for what they did wrong.

The life of Malala Yousafzai is a shining example of what's possible when we recognize a child's strengths. Malala is the young Pakistani activist who was shot in the head by the Taliban for speaking out for the right of girls to receive an education. For her brave advocacy she was awarded the Nobel Peace Prize in 2014. In his TED talk, "My Daughter, Malala"

(2014), Ziauddin Yousafzai speaks of the bold potential he saw in his daughter in a country where the birth of a girl is a disappointment. "I named her after Afghanistan's greatest freedom fighter and heroine, Malala Maiwand. When I looked in her eyes, I saw a light; I was extremely honored." Yousafzai had eyes that saw the best in his daughter.

Yousafzai, a human rights and women's rights activist himself, says, "I appreciated her intelligence and brilliance from a young age. I encouraged her to sit with me when my friends came to talk and to attend political meetings... At age four and a half, I admitted her in my school. In patriarchal societies (Pakistan), it is a big event for a girl to go to school. Admission in a school means a girl has an identity, a name, and that she has entered the world of dreams and aspirations." And that is how Yousafzai set the stage for his daughter's developing convictions and voice.

When Malala was eleven, the BBC contacted her father looking for a schoolgirl who would be willing to blog anonymously about life after being banned by the Taliban from attending school. Yousafzai volunteered Malala. "She is very articulate, more than me. ...She's a voice for all those girls who don't have a voice." With her father's faith in her, Malala blogged passionately about the restraints under Taliban rule. The BBC says of her blog, "It was one of the most popular blogs that we had done ... She had a huge audience, both local and international." Since her recovery, Malala has a much wider audience and influence as an advocate of education for all.

Malala's father recognized her intelligence, leadership qualities, and ability to express her thoughts powerfully. By seeing and describing her strengths to her often, he enabled her to capitalize on her abilities to effect change in their country and influence people profoundly all over the world.

To build your child's confidence:

- Choose a quality or two from your list and affirm your child often using the Four S's.

- Pass on compliments from others.

- Affirm your child's strength to others while in your child's earshot.

- Write notes of pride to leave on your child's pillow or in other places.

- Use the rubber band technique to remind yourself to affirm, not criticize.

Listen to Validate Their Thoughts and Feelings

The old saying, "Out of the mouth of babes..." hints at the insights, wisdom, and sometimes smack-on honesty our children possess. In my long career as a teacher, I discovered early on that students of every age have thoughts and ideas that are fresh, creative, and meaningful. We as adults have much to gain by listening with an open mind to the young. And when we listen with respect and curiosity to our children's thoughts, we dignify them.

Misty Copeland is the first African American soloist to dance with the prestigious American Ballet Theatre. In her autobiography, *Life in Motion: An Unlikely Ballerina,* she describes the life-changing impact of an adult's interest in her thoughts and opinions. When Misty was thirteen, she went to live with her ballet teacher, Cindy Bradley. Coming from a home with five siblings, Misty found it natural to remain quiet, in the background. But not so at the Bradley house. She says, "This was the first time I recall experiencing someone focused solely on me, attempting to hear what I had to say. Cindy would listen as though my conclusions were the wisest, most profound analyses she'd ever heard." Misty went on to reveal the impact of being fully listened to. "Without them (the Bradleys), I would not have learned to voice my opinion—to feel confident that I had opinions worth listening to."

Seek out your children's thoughts, opinions, reactions, and feelings. It will enrich your life, strengthen their confidence in expressing themselves, and make you closer to each other.

Listen Without Judgment to Create Trust

The older our kids get, the more challenging the situations they will be faced with. If we can listen without judgment, and encourage them to speak openly about what's going on with them and their peers, there's a better chance they will open up to us if they get into a sticky situation where they need our help the most.

Eileen, the mother of two boys, has an effective strategy for developing trust and deeper openness with her sons. When her older son, Dylan, was in eighth grade, she heard through the grapevine that one of his good friends was caught smoking an e-cigarette. Rather than react, she subtly opened the discussion with a question. "How's Robert doing?"

"He's OK, but guess what? He got caught with an e-cigarette."

Calmly Eileen probed to get Dylan thinking and to get more information herself. "Why do you think he's smoking?"

"I don't know, Mom. To be cool. That's why everyone does the things they do. Remember, his mom smokes, too."

"Would you ever try it?"

"I tried it once; it's not my thing."

At the end of Dylan's freshman year of high school, Eileen received a call that Dylan was caught smoking an e-cigarette. She went right to the school and picked him up. She didn't scream or yell, but linked her arm in his as they walked to the car.

"What's that for?" Dylan asked shakily.

"It's because I love you, and I'll always love you."

When they got in the car, Eileen said, "Now is your opportunity to tell me the whole truth."

"I was holding it for someone."

"Stop. Tell me the truth."

"OK. I bought it."

Eileen was convinced her conversation with Dylan the year before about e-cigarettes contributed to his willingness to be open with her now. She had been nonjudgmental then, and he trusted her not to overreact when he was truthful.

Once Dylan opened up, Eileen could explore the details of what, where, when, and how. Why would come later. She says about her strategy, "I begin gathering the facts. First, it's all concrete. My boys begin to open up as they tell the details. I don't react, I don't judge, I just listen and ask questions. After all the facts are out, I follow up with the why questions. These enabled me to understand Dylan's reasoning and gave me direction in terms of an appropriate consequence or support."

Besides grounding Dylan for two weeks and throwing out the e-cigarette, Eileen took a novel approach to help her son think more deeply about his choices. She had him fill out a questionnaire to reflect on the words others would use to describe him as a man someday, and whether his present behavior showed the person he wanted to be. As a result of this process, Dylan realized he wanted to be a healthier stronger person, and the whole family joined a gym.

Often when we deal well with challenges, there are surprisingly positive outcomes.

Keep the door to communication open between you and your kids by asking questions and being a nonjudgmental listener.

Appreciation Says You're Valued

Our kids are not merely dependent on us, they add to our lives. Their presence in the family makes a difference. In the movie, *It's a Wonderful Life,* Clarence the angel shares a poignant message: "Each man's (or woman's) life touches so many other lives. When he isn't around, it leaves an awfully big hole."

You are so right, Clarence. Think for a moment of the quirks and qualities your children bring to your family. Is it the way they make you laugh? Their flexible personality? Their stubborn determination? Curiosity? Helpfulness? What unique and invaluable contribution does your child make to your family? Showing your appreciation of who they are helps supercharge their journey toward a positive sense of self.

My sister has three grown daughters. Each feels she has a special place in her mother's heart. And each one does. Understanding their need to feel uniquely valued, Lois expresses her appreciation to each one in distinct, specific ways.

Her oldest daughter, Stephie, lives nearby and pushes my sister to walk a three-mile loop at the reservation near their homes each weekend. "Stephanie, I don't know what I'd do without you. I'd never exercise if you didn't push me. I'm so grateful for the way you motivate me."

Becky, her middle daughter, notices what needs to be done at family gatherings and pitches in without being asked. "Oy, my Becky. You give me such comfort with all your help. I can always count on you."

In Sami, her youngest, Lois appreciates that she visits at least once a month with her husband. They do yard work and fix things around the house. After they chopped and piled the wood from a fallen tree, Lois said, "Sami, what a good daughter you are. I couldn't imagine doing the work you're able to do. You're so handy."

Showing appreciation for our kids has double benefits: Our kids feel strengthened by their value reflected in our eyes, and we enjoy the pleasure of making them happy with our words of affirmation.

Motivate by Focusing on Their Effort

As parents, our dearest dream is that our kids will grow up to be happy and successful. We want to help them be the best they can be and even surpass us in every way. Words of motivation for our children are a powerful tool to help us make this dream a reality.

When I was a girl and during the first half of my teaching career, the common belief was that telling kids they're smart if they did well on a test, or were good if they behaved well, would build their self-esteem as learners. Not so, according to Stanford University motivation and mindset researcher, Carol Dweck. In her more than thirty years of studying student achievement, Dweck's findings show that kids who are repeatedly told they are smart are often afraid to take academic risks for fear of failing and looking stupid. That's not to say we don't recognize our kid's intelligence, but calling our kids smart doesn't help them tackle challenges and achieve more. Focusing on their effort does.

Effort is in our children's hands. If they work hard, they will discover they can improve. But merely saying to our kids, "Good try," won't build their sense of competence as a learner. In *The Atlantic* article, "How Praise Became a Consolation Prize: An Interview with Carol Dweck," Dweck cautions not to give empty praise to our children for just trying. "Students and our own children know that if they don't make progress and you're praising them, it's a consolation prize. They also know you think they can't do any better."

Dweck's latest research findings in *Education Week,* "Carol Dweck Revisits the 'Growth Mindset', clarifies effective ways to respond to our children's unsuccessful efforts so we can help them become confident in taking risks in their learning. Dweck advises us to encourage the following behaviors in our children:

- Experiment with different strategies to solve a problem
- Persevere through a difficult assignment
- Figure out what to do differently in the future
- Seek input when stuck

By naming and affirming these specific efforts when we see them in action, we support our kids in repeating these types of behaviors characteristic of successful people.

The following is an example of how specific feedback and affirmations about effort helped one student become a more competent and confident learner.

Randi, a student in Mrs. Myers' sixth-grade class, began the year in the advanced reading group. Her placement was based on her test scores and her strong analysis skills during large group discussions. But over the course of the first marking period, Mrs. Myers saw that Randi wasn't putting much thought into her reading responses, wasn't always prepared, and her work was careless. Randi's mother and her teacher put their heads together to come up with a plan to motivate her.

"In our large group reading discussions, you are focused and contribute meaningfully," Mrs. Myers said to Randi, "but in guided reading group your written work doesn't show much effort. I'm going to change your group. You can return to it when your work shows you belong there."

"What would it take to get back in the advanced reading group?" Randi asked.

Her teacher showed her examples of well-thought out, carefully written reading responses. Randi was inspired. She understood the kind of effort that would enable her to reach her goal.

At least once a week she checked in with her teacher to get feedback on her progress. "I got a three out of four on my reading response this week. How can I make it better?"

"You gave two good examples of the character's struggles. Now you need to connect those examples to how her struggles made her stronger." Mrs. Myers gave her some tips on extending her thinking and Randi went back to review the text and rework her response.

Right before the end of language arts period, Randi approached her teacher again with her reading response for feedback. "Is this better?"

After reading her work over Mrs. Myers said, "Not only did you show how the character's struggles made her stronger, I notice how serious you are in your commitment to improve. I can see you care about doing the best you possibly can do. You sought my help to understand how to more fully express your response, and you kept working at it until you were satisfied. Those are characteristics of successful learners."

Throughout the marking period, Randi worked diligently on her reading and writing assignments. The specific encouragement and affirmations she received from her teacher showed Randi how her efforts brought her the results she wanted. By the next marking period she achieved her goal.

Affirming the Difficult Child

Robert was a bright yet disrespectful student in my fifth-grade class. While I was telling the kids a story about Paul Revere's ride and the Revolutionary War, I'd see him roll his eyes, as if to say, "Who cares?" When I called on him later to explain his reasoning in solving a word problem, he said with a smirk, "It was easy, I don't need to explain it."

During read-aloud time, while I was animatedly reading the book *Wonder*, he was whispering behind his hand to a friend. "Robert," I said, "talking while I'm reading distracts me from doing my best reading for the rest of the class." He gave me an icy stare and shrugged his shoulders as if to say, "So what?"

There was an edge between Robert and me that needed addressing. I called his parents for a conference. His dad came in the next morning.

"Robert does very well on all his work," I said. "But he seems to have an attitude with me. He's being disrespectful, rolling his eyes, talking back, and giving me looks. Can you give me any insight about this?"

"You're right about Robert. He is smart, but he's also sensitive and holds his feelings in. After you called yesterday, I talked to him. He told me that he feels you don't like him because you seem to call on other kids more than him, but he absolutely shouldn't be disrespectful to you. I think he understands that now."

"You know, I feel your son has much to contribute to our class, and I'm going to sit down with him so we can talk and understand each other better."

I hadn't realized Robert was sensitive and felt he wasn't getting positive attention in class. At recess time I had him stay in so we could talk.

"I respect you tremendously as a student. You consistently do well on your assignments and you write so descriptively, it's as if we're there with you. Your writing would be a great model for other students."

"Really?" he asked warily.

"Definitely. The problem I'm having is with the looks you give me. It makes me feel you don't respect me and that upsets me."

With tears in his eyes in a hushed tone he said, "I didn't think you liked me. You always call on Cameron and Michael more than you call on me."

"That's because I know you understand the information and I'm trying to get students who need help to participate. My mistake. I would love to have you participate more."

At first, things were tenuous. I made it a point to call on him at least once during each subject, but he was still turning to his friends to whisper. I took him privately aside and asked, "How am I doing with calling on you more?"

"Good," he responded.

"I'm glad because I'm genuinely interested in your thoughts and ideas. They're helpful to your classmates, too. I notice you're not giving me looks anymore, and I

appreciate the way you're more respectful. I'm still noticing you whispering though, and that distracts me and the
other kids."

"Oh. Sorry."

The shift in attitude came gradually. I began using his
writing to teach tips to other students. "Notice how when
Robert says, 'I felt a butterfly attack in my stomach,' it grabs
our attention because we know the feeling." I could see
pleasure written all over his face.

I asked him, "Could you coach Cameron and Michael
for our social studies test? I know you understand the information and can explain it well."

"Sure," he answered with a smile.

Over the course of the year, I came to see a boy who
was a quick, insightful learner, a talented writer who was
willing to help his peers, and a good person. We developed
a positive relationship because he felt recognized and appreciated for his efforts and talents.

The young people in our lives rely on us to see the
best in them so they can see the best in themselves. Seeing
the best in our kids is not always easy or possible. We may
find them lazy, disrespectful, mean, bullyish, dishonest,
unwilling to listen, or unmotivated. But, being critical of
challenging kids doesn't serve them or us. How we talk to
them and about them will affect how our kids view themselves. When we recognize we're holding a negative view
of a child, it signals us to step back, get perspective, and
commit to understanding them better so we can see more
of who they are.

"It's good to remember your own pains, mistakes, and darkness," says Dr. Rachel Naomi Remen, who does this when she counsels others. Embracing all parts of herself enables her to connect to all parts of others.

As my fully imperfect self, I too have felt unrecognized, shame, helplessness, low self-esteem, and inferiority—feelings that might be behind a child's challenging behavior. This awareness triggers my compassion. I know any child who is acting out is probably feeling negative about himself.

Our role as adults is to help our kids to identify and accept their feelings so we can both start to focus on their strengths.

Is there a child with whom you've been butting heads that you'd like to shift the dynamics with?

What positive traits does he possess that you haven't been focusing on?

What might you do to support his strengths so he can rise to his better self?

How might you talk with him to open up communication?

How can you express responsibility for your part in the problem? Jot some ideas in your notebook.

The Gift of Positive Self-Talk

Imagine how much better life might be if from a young age we learned to speak to ourselves with positive words, rather than the stream of criticism so common for many of us.

Unrealistic expectations of perfection and critical self-judgments can make us unnecessarily hard on ourselves. Wouldn't it be nice to free our children from the burden of a negative inner voice? To shoo out that mean, old giant holding a club over their heads saying, "You're stupid!" *Bam!* "You screwed up again!" *Bam!* "You're not good enough!" *Bam!* Negative self-talk zaps energy, confidence, and makes any task harder.

Living the affirming way of life helps us create a new soundtrack of messages for ourselves and for our children. Through our affirming words we help our kids internalize a positive inner voice. "You used good judgment." *I did.* "You are responsible." *I am.* "That was so kind of you." *Yes it was.* Over time our words become their words. And there's more. Our kids pick up on how we talk about ourselves. As we practice being kinder and more understanding of ourselves, especially when we slip up, we model positive self-talk for our kids.

Model Positive Self-Talk

Twenty-three students sat on our colorful USA rug waiting for instructions. "Today, as I read aloud, we're going to work on the skill of drawing conclusions. Here's your sheet with questions to think about..." my voice trailed off. I'd

forgotten to copy the worksheet! My face felt like I was suffering from a nasty sunburn and my heart was pumping as
if I'd run a race. It's unnerving when you have twenty-three
pairs of expectant eyes on you—and you're unprepared.
Yet it was an opportunity to show my kids that nobody's
perfect, not even their teacher.

"Kids, I forgot to copy the questions for you. I feel a
little foolish, but we all make mistakes, right?" Some chuck-
led, others shook their heads affirmatively, and smiles
abounded. "I have to forgive myself though. This morning
I had to help Mrs. Mulleavey's substitute get ready for class.
Now what can we do? Any ideas?"

"How about no questions?" Remie suggested.

"Why don't we just read the chapters and you'll figure
out your own questions as we go along," Joe offered.

"I like Joe's idea," I said. "And kids, what I just did was
positive self-talk. Rather than call myself names for making
a mistake, I spoke kindly to myself and it was easier to solve
the problem. You can do that too."

I didn't set myself up as a perfect person who's always
in control. By showing them I make mistakes and can speak
kindly to myself, I opened the way for them to do the same.

Kristin Neff tells a wonderful story in her book *Self-Compassion* that shows how our children learn positive self-talk
through example. Her eight-year-old autistic son, Rowan,
had a harder time than most dealing with frustration because of his autism. To help him develop coping skills, she
regularly modeled speaking to one's self with kindness and
understanding. When he spilled water on himself and was

about to explode, she said in a comforting tone, "Poor dar-
ling, you spilled the water and got all wet. It's okay to be
upset and frustrated." Sometime later she saw her model-
ing of positive self-talk had taken root. As Rowan struggled
to remove a stuck DVD, she heard him say to himself, "It's
okay. Things break sometimes." There is no specific time
limit on how quickly our children learn from our model-
ing. What matters is our commitment to creating that positive inner soundtrack. Eventually, it becomes theirs.

Positive Self-Talk Phrases

Our negative voice is powerful. Remember it takes five affirmations to undo one nasty remark. So it's helpful to give
your kids an arsenal of positive phrases to combat the fa-
miliar negatives. Teach your kids what self-talk is and share
with them how you're working to strengthen your own
positive inner voice. The following are basic empowering
phrases to replace negative self-talk:

Negative	Positive
This is hard, I can't do it.	I know I can do this if I keep at it.
	I can do this.
	I've handled other hard things and I can do this too.
	I believe in myself.
Nobody likes me.	I'm a good person.
	I love myself.

I messed up. (failed effort)	I'm proud of myself for trying.
	I can learn from this.

If there's a particular negative phrase you hear your child repeating, you might want to have her choose a phrase from the positive list, write it on a note card, and hang it in a place where she will look at it often.

A difficult botany test gave me the opportunity to help a student I was tutoring become aware of self-talk. As we sat at my kitchen table, he vented, "Science sucks and I suck. I just don't get the connection of cellular respiration and photosynthesis! I'll never get it!" He shoved his textbook to the floor.

"I can see why. That is challenging stuff. But talking negatively to yourself isn't going to make it any easier." He breathed in deeply and his shoulders dropped. "I used to say negative things to myself too when I had difficulty with teaching. Things like, 'That was stupid! You just can't handle this,' and it just made whatever I was trying to do harder. I discovered if I talked more kindly and gently to myself, I could relax and find a solution more easily. If you were to talk more supportively to yourself, what might you say?"

"I dunno, maybe, 'You can do this; give it time.'"

"Sounds much better. Now what's another way you've studied successfully to learn new material?"

My student relaxed, came up with another study strategy, and got through photosynthesis. Each time we help our kids change their negative voice to a more encouraging one we bolster their inner strength.

Envision Your Kid's Best Life

This practice can be your icing on the cake as a parent. What dream or vision is more important than to see our kids leading happy, fulfilling, successful lives? The thoughts we think about our kids, just as much as the words we say to them, impact their present and their future. It's subtle but real. I know because I've seen the results in Theo's life and in my own.

The technique you're about to learn is a powerful way to create a positive mindset about our kids. It partners affirmation with envisioning.

When Theo was in high school and had to deal with teenage struggles, my vision went like this: *Theo has unshakeable self-confidence. He has loyal friends who are great kids. He is excelling at school. He loves his life.*

Each morning as I drove to work, I repeated these affirmations aloud with great enthusiasm and joy. With each affirmation, positive images of Theo's life filtered through my mind. By the time Theo was a junior, these positive visions indeed started becoming his reality. Here's how it happened.

The more I did this practice, the more my positive images of Theo's life became substitutes for the worries I would have otherwise focused on. When our kids struggle, we have angst, and our worry is often accompanied by negative images of their lives. When I envisioned Theo's happiness and success, my positive thoughts offset my concerns. They also prompted me to take action to assist him in places where he was struggling. First, I found him a good counselor. Then we fixed up our basement so he'd have a place to hang out with his friends. We were very intentional about helping Theo create the kind of life that made him happy. I give credit to the Universe for the rest.

I continue to envision a good life for him now that he's a young man in his twenties, but the focus has shifted. I say: *Theo lives his life with a passion; he loves his work and makes a difference in the world; he is married to the just right woman who's like a daughter to us; they have healthy wonderful children.* I always add, *he is protected by the bright white light; all his actions are guided by his highest self, for his highest good and the highest good of all those he comes in contact with.*

When I envision for my son, I don't try to control the specifics, like who his friends will be or where he'll work. That's his domain. I just consider the big areas of life—his health, his sense of self, his relationships, his work—and I imagine them all in the best possible light. I end with a blessing passed on to me by a spiritual mentor, *may this or something better be so.*

Focusing on life-affirming positives gives us the energy to guide our kids from a healthier place inside ourselves—a place that expects good things for them, rather than a place that's motivated by fear and worry.

What is your vision for your kids?

Is there an area where they are floundering or a goal that they desire you might create a positive vision statement for?

It might help to write down your visions so you can eventually memorize them as you are reciting and envisioning your child's best life. (For a reminder on creating affirmation statements go to Chapter 4.)

Be Patient, Be Real

Shifting perspective when you speak to your kids takes time. At first the words may feel unnatural, and if your kids are older, they may not trust what they're hearing. Nothing builds trust more than being real with kids. Tell them honestly that you've read this book and it's made you think more about the impact of your words on them. Tell them about your own experiences with criticism. Explain that you're working on being more positive, so if you sound a little weird, that's why. You can even ask for their feedback.

Your commitment to focus on and affirm the best in your kids will bring much happiness to both of you.

Your Takeaways

1. **Recognize your children's strengths and affirm them often.**

2. Appreciate the uniqueness and contribution each of your children brings to your family and tell them often.

3. Seek out your children's thoughts, feelings, reactions, and opinions.

4. Listen and ask questions without judgment to build trust between you and your children.

5. Motivate your kids by affirming them for their efforts. When their efforts are unsuccessful, recognize the actions they took to learn from their mistakes so they will have a repertoire of approaches to learn and improve.

6. Model and teach a kind, positive, self-talk voice that expresses forgiveness and acceptance for being human and making mistakes.

7. Envision your children's best life daily by repeating affirmations that bring positive thoughts and energy to their growth and dream fulfillment.

PART THREE

the Send-Off

CHAPTER 10

Taking Compliments In

At the end of the school year, Ben's mother stopped in my classroom with a gift and kind words. "You're the best teacher Ben has ever had. You saw the best in him and helped him see it, too. He's a much more confident student and loves reading now—all because of you."

"Thank you, Suzanne. He's who he is because you're such a great mother. You're so supportive and give him such a good life. We were a team this year." *Why can't I own that I was successful at helping Ben grow? Why can't I just say, "Thank you for your kind words. I'm so glad I reached your boy?"*

Taking affirmations in is not easy. We usually either deflect praise—sending it right back to the giver, or reject it—denying that we deserve the compliment. We need to learn to say thank you, smile, acknowledge, and appreciate the gift. Realize compliments are gifts from others, and our acceptance is a gift right back to them. Unfortunately, not all affirming words are well-intended. We need to recognize backhanded praise and handle it with respect for ourselves. The largest benefit of taking affirmations in is that they rewire our brain to focus on our own positive qualities, which fuels our affirmations of others and our happier life.

A Magnifier on How We Respond to Affirmations

In her memoir, *Year of Yes,* Shonda Rhimes, creator of *Grey's Anatomy,* one of my favorite TV shows, devotes a whole chapter to the challenge of taking compliments in and boldly owning our unique greatness. At an awards dinner celebrating women who've made major contributions in TV, Rhimes wryly observed that not one woman could own her powerful accomplishments. She says the honorees did one of three things: Some shook their head, waving off the applause as if to say, "Who me? What I did was no big deal. Anyone could have done it." Others ducked their heads in embarrassment as if to say, "Not me, I don't deserve the praise." And some laughed with a stunned expression as if to say, "How did I make it to the ranks of these great women? I'm not worthy."

Rhimes wonders, "What is our problem?" Whatever is going on with these highly accomplished women is going on with most of us. In fact, Christopher Littlefield, founder of Acknowledgments Works, and trainer of business leaders all over the world in the use of recognition in the workplace, substantiates that many of us have this problem. In his TEDxBeirut talk, "What Do You Want to Be Acknowledged For?" (2012), he describes the results of an experiment he conducted with this very question. For a full year, whether on the subway or a plane, Christopher asked the person sitting next to him, "What makes a good acknowledgment by a boss or supervisor?" Seventy percent of the more than 365 people interviewed said they found the compliments they received uncomfortable and embarrassing. But, why?

For many of us, it's enculturated. In the Greek language, if you say, "Thank you" (*efharisto*), the response is "Please" (*parakalo*), as if to say, "What I did is no big deal, no need for any acknowledgement." In French, it's the same. To "Thank you or *merci*," the response is "*De rien*," meaning, "No problem," or, "It's nothing." We learn by example that an appropriate response to compliments or an acknowledgement is to downplay our efforts.

Many of us deflect compliments. I am so guilty of this! Christopher Littlefield aptly calls this "compliment ping-pong." Often we deflect out of false humility—we don't want to look vain or come across as superior. Littlefield says, "Most of us know what it's like when someone else is recognized in a group while we aren't. For some of us, its jealousy. Having felt it ourselves, we know others might say things like, 'He's a kiss-ass, a jerk; he doesn't deserve it.'"

To counteract the anticipated criticism, we do like Rhimes and the other TV powerhouses, "Who me? Anyone could do what I do." It's easier to give the credit to the people who work with us. "It wasn't me. It was a team effort."

If we're not deflecting compliments, we may flat out reject them. Stephen Taylor, an online drumming teacher, tells a great story of an extreme rejection of a compliment. In a YouTube video "How to Accept a Compliment," Taylor describes how a musician he really respected came backstage after a gig to tell him and his band how much he enjoyed their show. "Man, you guys were great. You sounded even better than your album."

To which one of his band members replied, "You must have been listening to another guy."

"No, no, it was you."

"You obviously weren't there for the third song; it sucked."

"No, no, it was great."

Why do we sometimes put ourselves down when someone is offering us a lift up? Maybe it's because the affirmation doesn't match our self-perception. We may go out of our way, like the band member did, to prove the compliment is wrong. If our sense of self is low in a certain area, we may think the person is just trying to make us feel good.

How do you respond to compliments?

- *Are you a deflector?*

- *Do you give the credit to others or to luck?*

- *Are you a rejecter?*

- *Is a compliment too awkward to take in?*

- *Do you feel undeserving of it?*

- *It may be helpful to reflect on your response to compliments in your affirming notebook.*

Thank, Acknowledge, and Appreciate

Here is Stephen Taylor's simple three-step approach to respond to compliments graciously.

1. Smile and say, "Thank you."

    - A cheerful response opens the door to your heart and mind. Feel the good energy that is coming your way; better yet, bask in it. It's a gift not only from the individual complimenting you, but from the Universe saying you are valued and valuable.

2. Acknowledge the compliment: "I really appreciate you saying that."

    - The giver has affirmed you. Your acknowledgment returns the good feeling. It also gives the two of you a moment of positive connection with the potential to deepen your relationship.

3. Appreciate the compliment: "It means a lot to me that you would say…"

- Let the person know how much their words mean to you. Your response will vary depending on the substance of the compliment. For a compliment on your appearance you might simply say, "That makes me feel really good." A compliment for your performance at work might get a more substantial expression of appreciation like, "I worked hard on that presentation, and I'm so glad you were pleased with it."

My sister is a master at accepting compliments. She gives compliments out freely and joyfully receives them. The other day she told me a story about her experience with a new diabetes patient that perfectly illustrates using this thank-you approach.

The woman said to Lois, "I am here because my friend told me you are the best diabetes educator in the state. She said you are kind, knowledgeable, and an expert at teaching your patients how to manage their diabetes. You should go home, look in the mirror, and realize what an important person you are!"

"Thank you, that is so kind of you to say," Lois responded. "It makes me feel so good to hear that the way I teach about diabetes makes it easier for my patients. I will go home and do that. You made my day!" And it was true. My sister told me how this compliment filled her with joy and refueled her sense of purpose that her efforts were making a difference.

Not everyone is as comfortable receiving compliments as Lois is. When taking compliments in is new to you, it may feel awkward and unnatural. However, focusing on the meaning of the affirmation, especially from loved ones, can make a difference in how it feels. Denise Marigold, John Holmes, and Michael Ross of the University of Waterloo, Canada, in their *Journal of Personality and Social Psychology* article, "More Than Words: Reframing Compliments From Romantic Partners Fosters Security in Low Self-Esteem Individuals," found that when romantic partners were asked to describe the meaning and significance of a compliment from their loved one, they felt more positive about the compliment, themselves, and their relationship. The good feelings were still flowing even after two weeks.

I had the chance to see this process in action in the YouTube video, "The Power of Compliments/The Science of Love," presented by SoulPancake, a media company known for their positive and inspiring content. In the video, four couples show the effect of focusing on the meaning behind a compliment. One member of each couple was asked to write five authentic compliments about their partner. In the first round the receiving partner could only say thank you. In the second round the same compliments were repeated, but the receiver needed to express how each compliment made her feel and how it was significant to their relationship.

The first time Oscar said to Karina, "Because of who you are, I am inspired to be a better and stronger person on this planet," she blushed, smiled, and looked embarrassed as she said, "Thank you." The second time, though, it was clear that she really took the compliment in. Her eyes were shining, and her smile was in her cheeks and on her lips as she said, "I feel very thankful you think that way because I feel every day that you show me who I can be." At the end of the video we discover that based on a self-esteem pre- and post-test taken by receivers, appreciating the compliments they received increased their self-esteem up to thirty-four percent.

Gift to the Giver

When Oscar listened to Karina's response, his pleasure was apparent. As she expressed what his compliment meant to her, the love between them was palpable.

We usually don't think about our impact on people who compliment us, but if we did, we might realize expressing the significance of a compliment received is a gift to the giver as well as ourselves.

Sincere compliments may actually be more valuable than material gifts when we consider the deeper, long-lasting impact they can have on our lives. Greater confidence, self-acceptance, recognizing an unrealized talent, confirmation, feeling valued and respected, closeness with the giver—the benefits of taking compliments in are invaluable.

It takes courage, thought, and feeling to rouse the right words that express the positives we see in another person. Acknowledging and appreciating compliments says to the giver that you value their perspective, their generosity of spirit—you value them. And what's more, by warmly accepting their praise, you are encouraging them to continue complimenting you and others.

My friend Kathy was not by nature a complimenter. When I began sharing the drafts of these chapters with her, she explained that it just never occurred to her that her words impacted the people in her life, but seeing the warmth in my relationships made her interested in practicing the affirming way of life. On my birthday, I received a surprising call from her. She said, "You and Lois looked so gorgeous and relaxed in your Facebook pictures at the Boathouse. You both looked like movie stars! I'm so happy for you." Kathy had never complimented me like that before, and her words delighted me.

"Thank you so much. Your warm words mean so much to me. I really appreciate your call. Gorgeous is good!" Kathy's kind words and my heartfelt appreciation were bonding threads knitting us closer together. Kathy is affirming others more often now. The gift of affirming was not just for me.

Backhanded Compliments

Not all compliments are well-intended. Some can be backhanded—insults in disguise. The older generation of women on both sides of my family were blurters. They said whatever came to their minds without censor. It was my dad's sixtieth birthday. Eleanor threw him an elegant brunch at a French bistro in New York City. As we were mingling and drinking mimosas before the meal, Aunt Sarah, my dad's younger sister whom I hadn't seen in at least eighteen years, approached me. She was all smiles as she said, "Gail, I didn't recognize you. You look so pretty. Your skin has improved so much."

Of course it had. I was out of puberty. What did she expect? I was also thirty-five, had just ended my relationship with James, and was feeling quite vulnerable. Her comment felt like she had stomped her high heel deep into my exposed foot. How could my aunt, whom I hadn't seen in so many years, be so insulting?

I was so taken aback by her words that I didn't know what to say. I mumbled something and quickly excused myself to go help Eleanor. Though Aunt Lil had warned me about Aunt Sarah's sharp tongue, I was too inexperienced and insecure at the time not to be thrown by her backhanded compliment. The thing I did right, though, was to remove myself swiftly without becoming defensive, although I did later stew over her nastiness.

Living the affirming way of life reminds me to look from a larger perspective when I relate to other people. A backhanded compliment may reflect the other person's self-critical, perfectionist nature, and be more about the way they feel about themselves than me. I often remind myself, "Don't take it personally," as Don Carlos Ruiz advises in *The Four Agreements*. If we were just more educated about what to expect in situations from health to relationships, we might handle them so much better. Now, having greater confidence and more life experience, I would do a number of things differently with Aunt Sarah.

I might say, "Thanks. I have grown and changed a lot since we last saw each other," and then change the subject to focus on her. Or, "Thanks, Aunt Sarah, for saying I look pretty; that makes me feel good."

Our relationship with the person delivering the back-handed compliment, as well as our state of heart and mind, makes a difference in how their words feel. If my husband, who I know adores me, says, "You made a delicious dinner, I just wonder when you're going to iron all the clothes you've been piling up in our bedroom," I might respond playfully. "Oh, aren't you the persuasive one." I don't take his words personally. If I'm stressed though, I might call him out on it, "If you want the ironing done just say so, or, better yet, do it yourself!" Compliments have value when they make us feel valued. Maintaining our sense of worth, even in the face of twisted compliments, is essential because it is our own opinion of our self that matters most.

A Gift for You

Taking compliments in completes the full circle of living the affirming way of life. We give out positive energy; we get positive energy. We give strengthening words; we get strengthening words. We give encouragement; we get encouragement. We express gratitude; we receive gratitude. Not necessarily from the one we complimented, but it comes because of the flow we've created. Taking compliments in builds our positive sense of self, and gives us all the more good energy and good words to give out, enabling us to impact others far beyond what we might hope for.

By savoring the positives said to you, gradually you shift how you see yourself, other people, and all of life. You realize that you deserve to be valued, appreciated, and adored just because of who you are. And if that's true for you, it's also true for everyone else.

I cherish the following lines from Marianne Williamson's poem, "Our Deepest Fear," from her book *A Return to Love*. They beautifully crystallize why taking compliments in makes such a difference.

> We ask ourselves, "Who am I to be brilliant, gorgeous, talented, fabulous?'"
>
> Actually, who are you not to be?
>
> We are all meant to shine, as children do.
>
> We were born to make manifest the glory of God that is within us.
>
> It's not just in some of us; it's in everyone.
>
> And as we let our own light shine,
>
> We unconsciously give other people the permission to do the same.

Your Takeaways

1. **Notice how you respond to compliments. Are you a deflector? A reflecter? Make a commitment to take compliments in.**

2. Practice acknowledging compliments and appreciating the message. Say something like: "Thank you. That was kind of you. It makes me feel good that you noticed that about me."

3. Remember, a compliment is a gift, as much as any material item. Consider the giver's feelings when you receive a compliment.

4. Try these approaches with backhanded compliments: acknowledge the positive part; just say, "Thank you" and remove yourself from the situation; use humor; don't take what's said personally; and be sure to honor yourself.

5. Take compliments in. They rewire your brain with positive thoughts and feelings so you not only feel better, but also have more affirmations to give away.

CHAPTER 11

Say It Now

My ending story for you was gifted to me one summer morning while waiting for a FedEx drop-off facility to open. The customer service rep on the phone told me the facility nearest me opened at 9:30 a.m. When I arrived at 9:30 sharp, I noticed the sign on the sliding glass door said, "Saturday, open 10:00 a.m." Frustrating! With half an hour to kill, I decided to take a walk while the weather was still in the low eighties. The facility was in an industrial park on a long, grassy, tree-lined road. As I strolled enjoying the sun streaming through the trees, I asked God for the just right words to send you off, good reader, to live the affirming way of life.

At 9:57, I planted myself in front of the FedEx door. A woman joined me dressed in a sleeveless, bright orange running shirt with black running capris and sneakers.

"I've been here since 9:30, so I went for a half-hour walk to get my Fitbit steps in," I said.

"Yeah, I should go for my run, but I was out late last night and it's hard to get myself going."

"Well, you're dressed in your running clothes, so I bet some way you'll get yourself to do it."

"You're right," she answered. "You never regret taking positive action. You only regret when you don't."

"That's it! Thank you," I said filled with gratitude. "I was looking for the just right words to end my book and you just gave them to me!"

We usually live our lives as if we have infinite amounts of time. We treat our moments with others who are dear to us as if time will never run out. But now that I'm older and have had loved ones who've passed on, I know the preciousness of the moment.

Tim, from my favorite movie, *About Time,* knows too. With his power to go back to any time in his life, he redoes moments, days, or weeks to say and do things that help him marry the girl of his dreams and make a difference in the lives of people he cares about.

At the end of the movie, walking with his wife, carrying his two adorable daughters, Tim contentedly reflects to himself, *I now choose to live each day as if I am living it for a second time.* No regrets.

Tim's wisdom goes right to my heart. I wonder, *what would I do differently if this moment were all I had with a dear one?* I know and you know, I'd express my heart. So I ask you to ponder the same question. What would you want to say to the people you love and care about if you knew this moment were all you had with them? Are there words of love never said, appreciation unspoken, admiration held back?

Why not let loose and give it all away? Use all those positive feelings and words you've yearned to express but have hesitated to say. *Say it now.* You may not have the opportunity again.

I don't promise it will be easy being an affirmer. You may feel awkward at first. Your affirming words may not elicit a response you hope for or any response at all. Throw expectations out the window.

What I can assure you from my own experience is that as you focus on the good in others, you become a magnet for the good in yourself. Over time you will notice more of the good than the bad in people close to you and those you hardly know. Your perspective on life will shift, and your affirming words will impact others and your relationships in ways you can't even imagine.

As you continue living the affirming way of life, may you feel part of a larger plan, uplift the lives of others, and put good energy into the world. In so doing, may your relationships become closer, may your heart flow with love, and may you feel deep happiness and fulfillment. *Shoin!* (And so it is!)

References

Chapter 1: The Affirming Way of Life

1. Rick Hanson, *Hardwiring Happiness: The New Brain Science of Contentment, Calm, and Confidence* (New York: Harmony Books, 2013).

2. Gary Chapman, *The 5 Love Languages: The Secret to Love That Lasts* (Illinois: Northfield Publishing, 2010).

3. Andrew Newberg and Mark Robert Waldman, *Words Can Change Your Brain: 12 Conversation Strategies to Build Trust, Resolve Conflict, and Increase Intimacy* (New York: Penguin Group, 2012).

Chapter 3: Criticism

1. Stacey Finkelstein and Ayeltet Fishbach, "Tell Me What I Did Wrong: Experts Seek and Respond to Negative Feedback," *Journal of Consumer Research* 39(2012): 22-38.

2. Don Miguel Ruiz, *The Four Agreements* (California: Amber-Allen Publishing, 1997).

Chapter 4: Self-Supporting Words

1. Brené Brown, *The Gifts of Imperfection: Let Go of Who You Think You're Supposed to Be and Embrace Who You Are* (Minnesota: Hazelden, 2010).

2. Kristin Neff, *Self-Compassion: Stop Beating Yourself Up and Leave Insecurity Behind* (New York: HarperCollins, 2011), 61-76.

Chapter 5: Recognition Words

1. Simine Vazire and Erika N. Carlson, "Others Sometimes Know Us Better Than We Know Ourselves," *Sage Journals* (2011):104-108.

2. Marlo Thomas, *The Right Words at the Right Time* (New York: Atria, 2002), 374.

Chapter 6: Appreciative Words

1. Francesca Gino and Adam M. Grant, "A Little Thanks Goes a Long Way: Explaining why Gratitude Expressions Motivate Prosocial Behavior," *Journal of Personality and Social Psychology* 98 (2010): 946-955.

Chapter 7: Encouraging Words

1. Y. Joel Wong, "The Psychology of Encouragement: Theory, Research, and Applications," *The Counseling Psychologist* 43 (2015): 178-216.

2. Paula Beiger, *Guided Cure* (New Jersey: Self, 2016).

3. Langston Hughes, *The Dream Keeper: and Other Poems* (New York: Scholastic Inc., 1994), 64.

Chapter 8: Healing Words

1. Louise Hay, *You Can Heal Your Life* (California: Hay House, Inc., 1984), 221.

2. Robert Enright, *The Forgiving Life: A Pathway to Overcoming Resentment and Creating a Legacy of Love* (Washington DC: American Psychological Association, 2012).

3. Helen Schucman, *A Course in Miracles* (California: The Foundation for Inner Peace, 1976).

4. Julie Hall and Frank Fincham, "Self-Forgiveness: The Stepchild of Forgiveness Research," *Journal of Social and Clinical Psychology* 24 (2005): 621-637.

5. Rachel Naomi Remen, *Kitchen Table Wisdom: Stories That Heal* (New York: Riverhead Books, 1996), 143.

Chapter 9: Affirming Words for Our Children

1. Misty Copeland and Charisse Jones, *Life in Motion: An Unlikely Ballerina* (New York: Simon and Schuster, 2014), 79 and 134.

2. Neff, *Self-Compassion*, 218-220.

Chapter 10: Taking Compliments In

1. Shonda Rhimes, *Year of Yes: How to Dance it Out, Stand in the Sun, and Be Your Own Person* (New York: Simon & Schuster, 2015), 174-176.

2. Denise Marigold, John Holmes, and Michael Ross, "More Than Words: Reframing Compliments From Romantic Partners Fosters Security in Low Self-Esteem Individuals," *Journal of Personality and Social Psychology* 92 (2007): 232-248.

3. Ruiz, *The Four Agreements,* 47-61.

4. Marianne Williamson, *A Return to Love: Reflections on the Principles of A Course in Miracles* (New York: Harper Perennial, 1992), 190-191.

Acknowledgments

A cknowledging the love and support that enabled me to write this book means I get the chance to affirm the dear people in my life.

The first person I want to thank and affirm is my mother, Selma. She was such a kind, loving soul, and never received the honor she deserved in life. Mom, may this book honor you to the sky for being my role model for affirming. You have brought me, and all those whose lives I touch, great love and joy.

My wise and oh so supportive husband, Gus—you understood how much I wanted to be a writer and for years would say, "Write about what you know." Thank you, Honey, for your insightful advice and for always, always believing in me. I thank God for you every single day.

I am blessed with a sister like no other. Lois, you have been by my side my entire life, lifting me up through my rough patches and celebrating my joys as if they were your own. You have always been my role model for giving support and acceptance to others, and my affirming partner. This book is our shared message to the world.

Theo, you are just what your name means, *"Gift from God."* Being your mother has been the best and most important part of my life. Thank you for being so receptive to my affirmations and being the model for the amazing impact of affirming way of life parenting. I am so grateful to you for the nudge you gave me to take my first steps on the journey of writing this book.

My dearest friend-sister, Lynnie Spatzer, you have been my most dedicated reader. Thank you with all my heart for your interest, our deep conversations on each chapter, your honest feedback, and always believing in me.

My lifelong author-friend, Naomi Drew, you have inspired me throughout our friendship to grow in so many ways. I am grateful for your impeccable editing, all your guidance in fulfilling this dream, and always your friendship.

My teaching teammate and fellow adventurer, Kathy Mulleavey, I so appreciate your willingness to try the different forms of affirming and to share your stories of how much sweeter it made your life.

I'm so glad you came back into my life, Jamie Sussel Turner. Your generosity sharing publishing resources and all your experience getting the message out into the world have meant the world to me.

A thank you hug to my teamies, my last teaching teammates, who fanned my dream, practiced my ideas, and are the subject of many stories in the book.

My deep thanks to my post-teaching team, the Hamilton Writer's Group, led by Rodney Richards. You helped me to drop my lecturing, rose-colored glasses writing style, and to craft my words. Your feedback that my message was one you valued gave me faith that there was an audience for my ideas and confidence in myself as a writer.

My writing coach, Carol Kivler, if not for you I would still be starting stories and giving up. You generously took me on and helped me create a structure from which my message could emerge.

My content editor, Gay Norton Edelman, with your background in self-help books and your warm affirming spirit, you were the just right person to weed out the excess and help the essence of my message shine.

Thank you Sharron Stockhausen, my copyeditor, for patiently and good humoredly teaching me correct grammar as if I were in your university class. You gave the book the finishing touch it needed.

Ken Kowalski, friend, poet, retired teacher—I am so grateful for your time and thoughtful final reading of my book, I always feel lucky to have you and your wife Jerè in my corner.

Sherry Meyer, you were so kind to volunteer to be one of my proofers. Thank you for your invaluable, astute, detailed editing.

Sally Tazelaar, art teacher and talented artist—thank you for your beautiful cover design and always generous kind-hearted spirit. I so appreciate your willingness to take my idea and match the color and design to the feel of the book's message.

Joni McPherson, your creative interior design and graphics for the cover were just what I needed to attract my readers. Thank you for being so flexible and easy to work with.

To all my family, friends, students, their parents and colleagues–I thank you all for being in my circle of living the affirming way of life and our precious heart connections.

I love you all and feel graced to have each and every one of you in my life.

Share With Me Your Affirming Stories

If the affirming way of life struck a chord with you, as I hope it did, you are going to be affirming more and enjoying experiences that touch your heart and the hearts of your receivers. I'd love if you'd share your stories with me.

I am compiling a companion volume of readers' affirming stories as another source of inspiration. Your experience may be just what someone else needs to hear to find the courage to express appreciation, encouragement, or admiration. I'd be most grateful to have you join with me in spreading the affirming way of life.

Send stories to: gail@theaffirmingway.com.

Your contribution will be greatly appreciated!

More About Gail

Early on in her teaching career, Gail realized the powerful impact she had on young people's sense of self. In the classroom and beyond it became her life mission to use her words to strengthen and support others. Toward this end, for half her career she served as a peacemaking and conflict resolution specialist speaking and leading workshops for large audiences. Gail is a two-time Teacher of the Year award recipient.

Growing up with a bipolar mother, she has always been a seeker of spiritual and psychological insights to help her find peace amidst the chaos. Gail considers sharing these insights through the affirming way of life approach to living her legacy to spread more positive energy in the world. Gail and her family enjoy trips to Greece to her husband, Gus's mountain village, Anavryti.

To learn more about Gail's work and to keep up with her blog, visit her website www.theaffirmingway.com. You can contact her for talks, workshops, and readings at gail@theaffirmingway.com.

Made in the
USA
Middletown, DE